CHARLOTTE & PETER FIELL

CHARLES RENNIE MACKINTOSH

1868– 1928

TASCHEN

KÖLN LONDON LOS ANGELES MADRID PARIS TOKYO

© 2004 TASCHEN GmbH
Hohenzollernring 53, D–50672 Köln
www.taschen.com

Original edition: © 1995 Benedikt Taschen Verlag GmbH
Edited by Thomas Berg, Bonn; Angelika Muthesius, Cologne
Co-edited by Yvonne Havertz, Cologne
Designed by Mark Thomson, London; Thomas Berg, Bonn;
Claudia Frey, Cologne
Cover design by Mark Thomson, London; Angelika Muthesius, Cologne
German translation by Maria Poelchau, Hamburg (essay);
Hans Heinrich Wellmann, Hamburg (descriptions)
French translation by Françoise Treuttel, Paris

The pictorial material published here for the first time
was photographed by Anthony Oliver, London.

Printed in Italy
ISBN 3-8228-3204-9

INHALT | CONTENTS | SOMMAIRE

6   Charles Rennie Mackintosh (1868–1928)

46   Glasgow Herald Building
48   Martyrs' Public School
50   Buchanan Street Tea Rooms
52   Glasgow School of Art
64   Argyle Street Tea Rooms
68   Competition for the 1901 Glasgow International Exhibition Buildings
70   Queen's Cross Church
72   120 Mains Street
76   Installation for the Eighth Secessionist Exhibition, Vienna
78   Windyhill
82   Ingram Street Tea Rooms
86   Competition for the Haus eines Kunstfreundes
92   14 Kingsborough Gardens
94   Installation for the International Exhibition of Modern Decorative Art, Turin
98   Competition for the Liverpool Anglican Cathedral
100   Wärndorfer Music Salon
102   Hill House
112   Willow Tea Rooms
122   Installation for the Dresdener Werkstätten für Handwerkskunst Exhibition
124   Hous'hill
130   Scotland Street School
136   Auchenibert
138   6 Florentine Terrace
142   78 Derngate
146   Project for Studio Houses
148   Project for a Block of Studio Flats for the Arts League of Service

150   Textile Designs | Textildesigns | Tissus d'ameublement

158   Watercolours | Aquarelle | Aquarelles

168   Chronology | Chronologie
174   Notes | Anmerkungen
175   Bibliography | Bibliographie
175   Acknowledgements | Danksagung | Remerciements
176   Credits | Bildnachweis | Crédits

CHARLES RENNIE MACKINTOSH (1868–1928)

Charles Rennie Mackintosh (1868–1928), architect, designer and artist, is an even more enigmatic figure today than when he was alive. While the astonishing modernity of his work has long ensured him a place of prominence among the pioneers of the Modern Movement, in recent years, his promotion of symbolic decoration has been hailed as prophetically post-modern. This intriguing dichotomy has not only compounded the enigma surrounding Mackintosh, it has also obscured the significance of the humanist intentions underlying his methodology.

Despite being remembered more often as a designer of furniture, due no doubt to his immense output of over four hundred furniture designs throughout his professional career, Mackintosh was first and foremost an architect. He believed that architecture was the supreme discipline, for it uniquely brought all the arts together. To understand the essence of his work, each of his architectural and interior projects must be considered as complete organic unities in which the whole was very much more important than the sum of the individual parts. He aimed to connect individuals with his work both functionally and spiritually, and believed that this could be achieved through a holistic approach to architecture and design which included the appropriate use of symbolism and the careful balancing of opposites: modernity with tradition, the masculine with the feminine, light with dark, and the sensual with the chaste. The work he produced possesses not only an inherent tension but a distinctive character that is as compelling and perplexing as the story of his own life, which reflects his position as a figure ahead of his time caught in the difficult transition between the Victorian era and the Modern Age.

Charles Rennie Mackintosh, c. 1900

THE EARLY YEARS

Charles Rennie Mackintosh was born in Glasgow on 7 June 1868, the second son in a family of eleven children. His father, William McIntosh[1], was a police superintendent in Glasgow—a relatively high position within the constabulary—and a Highlander. His mother, Margaret, was a Lowlander and from all accounts a mild-mannered, home-loving woman who was adored by her children.

Initially, the family lived in a tenement flat at 70 Parson Street in the East End of Glasgow; around 1878 they moved to a house at 2 Firpark Terrace, Dennistoun, a leafy suburb of the city. William McIntosh was a keen gardener and encouraged his children to participate actively in his hobby. This early exposure to horticulture led Mackintosh to a deep appreciation of nature, from which his organic approach to design evolved; an approach which employed Symbolist vocabulary to translate the forms found in the natural world into his designs. Indeed,

Der Architekt, Designer und Maler Charles Rennie Mackintosh (1868–1928) erscheint heute noch rätselhafter als zu seinen Lebzeiten. Die erstaunliche Modernität seines Werks hat ihm schon lange eine herausragende Stellung unter den Pionieren der klassischen Moderne gesichert, und in den letzten Jahren wird er wegen seiner symbolischen Formensprache sogar als Vorläufer der Postmoderne gewürdigt. Die Konzentration auf diesen faszinierenden Doppelaspekt in Mackintoshs Werk hat das Rätselhafte seiner Persönlichkeit in den Vordergrund gestellt, gleichzeitig aber die zutiefst humanistischen Bestrebungen vernachlässigt, die seinem Werk zugrunde lagen.

Auch wenn man Mackintosh vielleicht eher als Möbeldesigner in Erinnerung hat, was zweifellos an seinen mehr als vierhundert Möbelentwürfen liegt, war Mackintosh doch zuerst und vor allem Architekt. Er hielt die Architektur für die höchste Disziplin, weil sie alle Künste auf einzigartige Weise miteinander zu verbinden vermag. Um das Wesentliche seiner Arbeit zu verstehen, muß man jedes seiner Architektur- und Inneneinrichtungsprojekte als organische Einheit betrachten, bei der das Ganze wichtiger ist als die Summe der Bestandteile. Ihm ging es darum, zwischen den Menschen und seinem Werk eine sowohl funktionale als auch geistige Verbindung herzustellen. Er glaubte, dies durch eine ganzheitliche Auffassung von Architektur und Design erreichen zu können, die eine angemessene Verwendung von Symbolik und den behutsamen Ausgleich von Gegensätzen einbezieht: von Modernität und Tradition, Männlichem und Weiblichem, Hellem und Dunklem, Sinnlichkeit und Askese. Sein Werk besitzt nicht nur innere Spannung, sondern auch einen unverwechselbaren Charakter und ist ebenso fesselnd und frappierend wie seine Lebensgeschichte, die seine historische Stellung spiegelt: eine Gestalt, die ihrer Zeit voraus und zugleich in dem schwierigen Übergang zwischen der Viktorianischen Zeit und der Moderne befangen ist.

DIE FRÜHEN JAHRE

Charles Rennie Mackintosh wurde am 7. Juni 1868 in Glasgow als zweiter Sohn einer Familie von elf Kindern geboren. Sein Vater, der Highlander William McIntosh[1], hatte als Hauptkommissar in Glasgow eine relativ hohe Position im Polizeidienst inne. Seine Mutter Margaret stammte aus den schottischen Lowlands und war allen Berichten zufolge eine sanfte, häusliche Frau, die von ihren Kindern über alles geliebt wurde.

Die Familie lebte zunächst in einer Mietwohnung in der Parson Street 70 im Osten von Glasgow. Um 1878 bezog sie das Haus Firpark Terrace 2 in Dennistoun, einem grünen Vorort. William McIntosh war ein leidenschaftlicher Gärtner und hielt seine Kinder an, sich aktiv an seinem Hobby zu beteiligen.

Charles Rennie Mackintosh (1868–1928), architecte, designer et peintre, est encore plus mystérieux aujourd'hui qu'il a pu l'être de son vivant. L'étonnante modernité de son œuvre lui assure depuis longtemps une place au premier rang des pionniers du Mouvement Moderne. Et depuis quelques années, on salue en lui un maître de l'ornementation symboliste et donc un précurseur du post-modernisme. Cette étrange contradiction épaissit encore le «mystère Mackintosh», elle masque le sens profond des intentions humanistes qui sous-tendent la démarche créatrice de l'homme.

Bien que plus connu comme créateur de mobilier, sans doute à cause de sa production considérable (plus de 400 projets sur toute sa carrière), Mackintosh était avant tout architecte. Il pensait que l'architecture était la discipline suprême, la seule à rassembler tous les arts. Pour comprendre l'essence de son œuvre, il faut considérer que chacun de ses projets, qu'il soit architectural ou de décoration intérieure, est une unité organique complète dans laquelle l'ensemble est beaucoup plus que la somme des parties. Mackintosh voulait donner à son œuvre une dimension à la fois fonctionnelle et spirituelle, grâce à une approche globale de l'architecture et du design, associant symbolisme et équilibre des contraires: modernité-tradition, masculin-féminin, lumière-ombre, sensualité-chasteté. Cette tension se retrouve dans son œuvre. On y découvre aussi une singularité qui fascine et intrigue autant que l'histoire de sa vie, et qui reflète sa position de précurseur à une époque de transition entre l'ère victorienne et l'âge moderne.

LES PREMIÈRES ANNÉES

Charles Rennie Mackintosh, né à Glasgow le 7 juin 1868, était le deuxième fils d'une famille de onze enfants. Son père William McIntosh[1] venait des *Highlands*; il était inspecteur de police à Glasgow—un poste relativement important dans cette ville. Sa mère Margaret était née dans les *Lowlands*. Aux dires de tous, c'était une femme d'intérieur douce et adorée de ses enfants.

Les Mackintosh vécurent d'abord en appartement, dans un immeuble de rapport au 70 Parson Street, dans l'East End de Glasgow. Vers 1878, ils s'installèrent dans une maison au 2 Firpark Terrace à Dennistoun, un faubourg verdoyant de Glasgow. William McIntosh consacrait beaucoup de temps au jardinage et encourageait ses enfants à l'aider. Ce contact précoce avec l'horticulture développa chez Charles Rennie un sens profond de la nature où il puisera son esthétique «organique». Grâce au vocabulaire symboliste, il parviendra à traduire dans ses réalisations la richesse de la nature. La meilleure preuve de l'influence de la nature sur son œuvre se trouve dans ses projets d'architecture, dont le dynamisme évoque celui des organismes vivants.

the extent to which nature informed Mackintosh's work is best demonstrated in his subsequent architectural projects, which possess a dynamism akin to that of living organisms.

Charles Rennie Mackintosh was a weak child, having been born with a contracted sinew in one foot which left him with a pronounced limp—a disability that was referred to in an account by Lady Alice Barnes as a "clubfoot"[2]. During his childhood, he also suffered a chill in the muscles of his right eye which caused a permanent droop. The family doctor instructed his parents that "the boy should be encouraged to take plenty of exercise in the open air and to have long holidays whenever possible"[3]. The family therefore took annual vacations throughout Scotland, and Charles also enjoyed frequent "strengthening" rambles in the countryside surrounding Glasgow, sketching the buildings, flora and fauna that he came across. These trips not only had a beneficial effect upon his health, they also instilled in him, while young, a deep appreciation of the cultural heritage of his native land and a great sense of patriotism that remained with him throughout his life.

As a boy, Mackintosh did not particularly excel at either of the two schools he attended: Reid's Private School and later, Alan Glen's High School. It has been suggested that he suffered from "specific developmental dyslexia", a condition of physical origin often associated with high intelligence and heightened creative skills.[4]

From an early age, he expressed a desire to become an architect and, ignoring the wishes of his father, he became articled at the age of sixteen to the architectural firm of John Hutchison. At the end of his apprenticeship in 1889, he left Hutchison's and joined the newly formed partnership of John Honeyman and John Keppie to work, at first, as a draughtsman. During these formative years, there were many influences that had a direct bearing upon Mackintosh's professional development. These ranged from the secular (such as marine engineering and the Scottish Baronial style) to the spiritual (Japanese design and architecture, and the pantheism of Celtic belief), and mirrored his interest in both the national and international.

Mackintosh's name has become synonymous with his native Glasgow and is evocative of the city's illustrious past. At the turn of the century, such was Glasgow's industrial and economic might—a result of the thriving shipbuilding industry along the banks of the River Clyde and the nearby coal and mineral mines—that it had become the sixth largest city in Europe and was popularly known as "the Second City of the Empire". It is not surprising, therefore, that a strong sense of civic pride existed among Glaswegian industrialists. Low rates of income tax and the non-taxation of company profits encouraged a high level of artistic patronage. Their

Diese Erfahrungen weckten in Mackintosh eine tiefe Liebe zur Natur, auf deren Grundlage er später sein organisches Design und seine symbolistische Formensprache entwickelte. Der Einfluß der Natur auf Mackintoshs Werk zeigt sich besonders deutlich in der organischen Dynamik seiner späteren Architekturprojekte.

Charles Rennie Mackintosh war ein schwächliches Kind. Wegen einer angeborenen Sehnenverkürzung im Fuß hinkte er stark—eine Behinderung, die von Lady Alice Barnes als „Klumpfuß"[2] bezeichnet wurde. In seiner Kindheit zog er sich zudem eine Entzündung des rechten Augenmuskels zu, die zu einem Hängelid führte. Der Hausarzt riet den Eltern, „den Jungen zu ausgiebiger Bewegung in frischer Luft anzuregen und ihm, so oft es geht, lange Ferien zu ermöglichen"[3]. So machte die Familie Mackintosh jedes Jahr in verschiedenen Gegenden Schottlands Urlaub; außerdem unternahm Charles häufig „kräftigende" Streifzüge in die ländliche Umgebung Glasgows und zeichnete unterwegs, was er sah: Häuser, Flora und Fauna. Diese Ausflüge kamen nicht nur seiner Gesundheit zugute, sondern erweckten in ihm frühzeitig eine tiefe Liebe zu dem kulturellen Erbe seiner Heimat und starke patriotische Gefühle, die ihn sein Leben lang nicht losließen.

Als Schüler der Reid's Private School und danach der Alan Glen's High School tat Mackintosh sich nicht besonders hervor. Man nimmt an, daß er an einer „entwicklungsspezifischen Legasthenie" litt, einer physisch bedingten Störung, die oft mit hoher Intelligenz und außergewöhnlichen schöpferischen Fähigkeiten einhergeht.[4]

Von frühester Jugend an äußerte Mackintosh den Wunsch, Architekt zu werden, und gegen den Willen seines Vaters trat er mit sechzehn Jahren als Praktikant in das Architekturbüro von John Hutchison ein. 1889 verließ er nach Beendigung seiner Lehrzeit diese Firma und fing bei dem neugegründeten Büro von John Honeyman und John Keppie als Entwurfszeichner an. Während dieser Ausbildungsjahre haben viele Einflüsse auf Mackintoshs berufliche Entwicklung eingewirkt. Sie reichen vom Profanen bis zum Spirituellen, vom Schiffbau und dem schottischen Feudalstil bis hin zu japanischem Design und japanischer Architektur sowie die keltischen Götterwelt und spiegelten sein Interesse an nationalen wie internationalen Strömungen wider.

Mackintoshs Name ist gleichsam zu einem Synonym seiner Heimatstadt Glasgow und ihrer glanzvollen Vergangenheit geworden. Um die Jahrhundertwende hatte sich Glasgow—infolge des florierenden Schiffbaus an den Ufern des Clyde, der Eisenhütten und Kohlenbergwerke in der näheren Umgebung—zur sechstgrößten Stadt Europas entwickelt und wurde im Volksmund „die Zweite Stadt des Empire" genannt. Es überrascht daher nicht, daß Glasgower Industrielle einen ausgeprägten Bürgerstolz an den Tag legten. Infolge der niedrigen Einkommensteu-

Charles Rennie Mackintosh était un enfant maladif. Il souffrait d'une malformation congénitale à un pied qui le faisait boiter. (Lady Alice Barnes parle de «pied-bot»[2]). Il fut également victime d'un refroidissement musculaire qui lui laissa une paupière tombante. Le médecin de famille recommanda l'exercice en plein air et de longues vacances.[3] C'est ainsi que les McIntosh se mirent à visiter l'Ecosse. Le jeune Charles profita de ses promenades «fortifiantes» dans la campagne autour de Glasgow pour dessiner les plantes, les animaux, les maisons. Ces excursions eurent un effet bénéfique sur sa santé, et lui firent apprécier très tôt le patrimoine culturel de son pays natal. Elles développèrent aussi en lui un patriotisme dont il ne se départira jamais.

Mackintosh ne fut pas particulièrement bon élève dans les deux écoles qu'il fréquenta: la Reid's Private School et plus tard la Alan Glen's High School. Il souffrait apparemment d'une «forme particulière de dyslexie», trouble d'origine physique souvent associé à une grande intelligence et à une puissante créativité.[4]

Mackintosh exprima dès l'enfance le désir de devenir architecte. Passant outre à l'opposition de son père, il se fit engager comme apprenti à seize ans dans l'agence d'architecture de John Hutchison. En 1889, à la fin de son apprentissage, il quitta Hutchison et fut engagé comme projeteur dans l'agence que John Honeyman et John Keppie venaient de créer. Au cours de ces années de formation, Mackintosh s'imprégna de toute une série d'influences, tant techniques—la construction navale et le style «féodal écossais»—que spirituelles—la décoration et l'architecture japonaise, le panthéisme celtique— qui toutes témoignent de l'intérêt qu'il portait à son pays et au monde.

On ne peut aujourd'hui citer le nom de Mackintosh sans penser immédiatement à Glasgow, et sans évoquer le passé illustre de cette ville. Au début du siècle, Glasgow était à l'apogée de sa puissance industrielle et commerciale, grâce au boom de la construction navale sur les rives du Clyde et à l'exploitation des mines de charbon et de fer toutes proches. Elle était devenue la sixième métropole d'Europe, et on la surnommait «la seconde ville de l'Empire». Naturellement, les industriels de Glasgow étaient très fiers de leur ville. Le faible taux d'imposition des revenus et la non-imposition des bénéfices industriels encourageaient le mécénat. D'imposants bâtiments en grès de style néo-classique —le Kelvingrove Museum and Art Gallery, entre autres—témoignent de la puissance marchande de Glasgow à cette époque.

Les anciens étudiants en architecture trouvant de plus en plus de débouchés dans les chantiers navals, la Glasgow School of Art adopta un programme d'études qui préparait davantage aux métiers de la construction navale et de l'ingénierie qu'aux métiers artistiques proprement dits. En 1884, Mackin-

The Clyde, Glasgow, from sailors' home, c. 1900
Blick vom Seemannsheim auf den Fluß Clyde, Glasgow
Le Clyde, Glasgow, vue depuis une maison de marin

Charing Cross, Glasgow, 1901

colour."[6] Similarly, Mackintosh's buildings can be seen as the concrete expression of Lethaby's credo, encapsulated in his 1892 book *Architecture, Mysticism and Myth*, that "at the heart of ancient building there was wonder, magic and symbolism; the motive of our [buildings] must be human service, intelligible structure and verifiable science"[7].

Because of his successes in South Kensington and in local competition, Mackintosh's name was kept before the public. As a result, he was invited in February 1891 to deliver a paper entitled *Scottish Baronial Architecture* at the Glasgow Architectural Association—borrowing liberally from recently published texts by W. R. Lethaby and David MacGibbon and Thomas Ross.[8] Here, Mackintosh celebrated Scotland's native architecture, linking the virtues of its traditional values to the design issues of his day. For him, the "leading historical claims" of the Scottish Baronial style were that it was inherently "modern" due to its functionalism, that it was the last true native style of his country unsullied by classicism, that it had a stronger national identity than any style preceding it, and that it was the pre-eminent architectural legacy of his nation's forefathers and land. He commended the "extraordinary facility of our style in decorating, constructing, and in converting structural and useful features into elements of beauty"[9].

From his earliest designs, such as his contribution to the Glasgow Herald building (ill. pp. 46–47), this marriage of local tradition and a far-sighted Modernism can be recognized. In common with his contemporaries who were aligned to the Arts & Crafts Movement, he believed that decoration should avoid artifice and be used only within an appropriate context for symbolic purpose. Throughout his career and especially in his white, highly feminine interiors, Mackintosh repeatedly made reference to roses, symbolizing love, which to him was the fountainhead of life. Another favourite motif was the dove, symbolizing peace, which was used in the tranquil interiors of Queen's Cross Church and his own bedroom at 6 Florentine Terrace (ill. pp. 138–141).

One of the most significant differences, however, between Mackintosh and the proponents of the English Arts & Crafts Movement, was that he did not promote craftsmanship for its own sake. Indeed, it was more important to Mackintosh that his furniture should make a strong visual statement, giving coherence to an interior, than embody handcraft virtuosity and a preoccupation with function. The overall aesthetic was his primary concern rather than the technical means of achieving it. Mackintosh, therefore, must be considered as having been only loosely associated with the Arts & Crafts Movement. Although he was also one of the primary influences on the Art Nouveau style, he was not directly aligned to it either, for he rebuked the use of ornament for purely decorative purposes.

moderne Gewänder kleiden—unsere Entwürfe mit lebendiger Phantasie ausschmücken. Wir brauchen Entwürfe von lebenden Menschen für lebende Menschen—Werke, die das Heilige, individuell, Kunstfertigkeit, Freude an der Natur, an anmutiger Form und fröhlicher Farbe spiegeln."[6] Mackintoshs Bauten können als konkrete Ausformung des von Lethaby in seinem Buch *Architecture, Mysticism and Myth* 1892 formulierten Glaubensbekenntnisses gelten: „Tief im Inneren der Baukunst des Altertums herrschten Wunder, Magie und Symbolik; die unsere muß vom Dienst an der Menschheit, von erkennbarer Struktur und überprüfbarer Wissenschaft ausgehen."[7]

Seine Erfolge beim South Kensington Museum und bei lokalen Wettbewerben machten Mackintosh bald bekannt. So wurde er im Februar 1891 von der Glasgower Architektenkammer eingeladen, einen Vortrag mit dem Titel *Scottish Baronial Architecture* zu halten, in dem er freizügig aus kurz zuvor veröffentlichten Texten von W. R. Lethaby, David MacGibbon und Thomas Ross[8] zitierte. In diesem Vortrag rühmte er die schottische Architektur und verband deren traditionelle Werte mit den Erfordernissen der Baukunst seiner Zeit. In seinen Augen kam dem schottischen Feudalstil ein historischer Führungsanspruch zu, weil er aufgrund seiner Funktionalität von Natur aus „modern" und der letzte wahrhaft einheimische, vom Klassizismus nicht beeinflußte Stil sei; zudem besitze er eine stärker ausgeprägte nationale Identität als jeder vorangegangene Stil und stelle das herausragende architektonische Vermächtnis Schottlands dar. Er empfahl die „außergewöhnliche Eignung unseres Stils zum Dekorieren, Bauen und zum Umwandeln struktureller und nützlicher Elemente in schöne Formen"[9].

Diese Verschmelzung einheimischer Tradition mit einem weit vorausschauenden Modernismus läßt sich schon in Mackintoshs frühesten Entwürfen wie seinem Beitrag zum Gebäude des Glasgow Herald (Abb. S. 46–47) erkennen. Wie seine auf die Arts-and-Crafts-Bewegung eingeschworenen Zeitgenossen glaubte er, daß das Dekor jedwede Künstlichkeit vermeiden und lediglich im entsprechenden Umfeld zur Symbolik genutzt werden solle. In seinem gesamten Werk, besonders in seinen weißen, betont femininen Inneneinrichtungen nutzte Mackintosh wiederholt das Motiv der Rosen, um die Liebe zu symbolisieren, für ihn der Quell des Lebens. Ein anderes Lieblingsmotiv war die Taube als Friedenssymbol, das er in der Queen's Cross Church und in seinem Schlafzimmer in Florentine Terrace 6 verwendete (Abb. S. 138–141).

Einer der wichtigsten Unterschiede zwischen Mackintosh und den Verfechtern der englischen Arts-and-Crafts-Bewegung bestand darin, daß er das Kunsthandwerk nicht um seiner selbst willen förderte. Ihm kam es mehr auf den optischen Eindruck seiner Innenausstattungen, auf die Geschlossenheit

Aubrey Beardsley:

Lysistrata haranguing the Athenian Women, lithograph, 1896

Lysistrata hält eine flammende Rede vor den Frauen Athens, Lithographie

Lysistrata haranguant les Athéniennes, lithographie

MacGibbon et Thomas Ross[8] qui venaient de paraître. Dans cette conférence Mackintosh vante cette architecture née en Ecosse, et établit un lien entre les vertus de la tradition et les nouvelles exigences de la modernité. A l'en croire, «les droits historiques» du style féodal écossais étaient les suivants: il était foncièrement «moderne» par son fonctionnalisme; c'était le dernier style indigène écossais à ne pas avoir été perverti par le néo-classicisme; il manifestait mieux que tous ceux qui l'avaient précédé le caractère national; et enfin il symbolisait l'héritage légué par les ancêtres et la nation écossaise. Mackintosh notait aussi d'«extraordinaire aisance de ce style, quand il s'agit de décorer, construire ou transformer des éléments structurels et techniques en formes belles».[9]

Ses premiers projets, telle sa contribution à l'immeuble du Glasgow Herald (ill. p. 46–47), marient tradition locale et modernité d'avant-garde. A l'instar de ses contemporains du mouvement Arts & Crafts, il estime que la décoration doit éviter l'artifice, n'être utilisée qu'à bon escient et à des fins d'expression. Tout au long de sa carrière, mais surtout dans ses intérieurs féminins blancs, Mackintosh utilise la rose comme motif: elle symbolise l'amour, source de vie. Un autre de ses motifs de prédilection est la colombe, symbole de paix. On la trouve en particulier à la Queen's Cross Church de Glasgow et dans sa chambre à coucher du 6 Florentine Terrace (ill. p. 138–141).

Mais Mackintosh se différencie des membres du mouvement Arts & Crafts dans la mesure où il ne défend pas l'artisanat en tant que tel. Il voulait que son mobilier fasse une forte impression visuelle et donne à une pièce son unité, plutôt que de manifester la virtuosité technique ou le souci de fonctionnalité de son créateur. Il recherchait la beauté d'ensemble plutôt que les moyens techniques d'y parvenir. On peut en conclure que ses liens avec le mouvement Arts & Crafts ont été relativement ténus. Important précurseur de l'Art nouveau, il ne s'en distingue pas moins par son refus de l'ornement à des fins purement décoratives. Mackintosh est avant tout un créateur profondément original; il est resté en dehors des grands courants stylistiques de son temps.

Mackintosh a su puiser à des sources variées qu'il a combinées pour créer un vocabulaire et un style originaux. A cet égard, le symbolisme de son œuvre doit beaucoup à l'art celtique. C'est en particulier le cas de ses premières aquarelles: *The Tree of Personal Effort* (L'Arbre de l'Effort Personnel, ill. p. 162) et *The Tree of Influence* (L'Arbre de l'Influence, ill. p. 162). Mackintosh partageait le respect païen des Celtes pour le monde naturel. Panthéistes, ils vouaient notamment un culte aux arbres, auxquels ils attribuaient des vertus humaines: c'est ainsi que le chêne personnifiait la force. L'élément central de la mythologie celtique était «Craobh an Eolais» ou

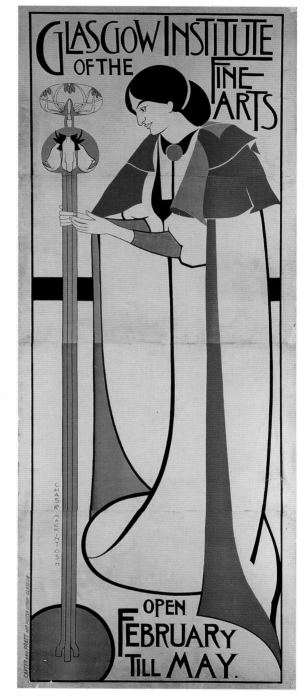

Poster for the *Glasgow Institute of the Fine Arts*, colour lithograph, 1895
Plakat für das *Glasgow Institute of the Fine Arts*, Farblithographie
Affiche pour le *Glasgow Institute of the Fine Arts*, lithographie en couleur
223.8 x 89 cm

Mackintosh was an intensely individualistic designer and must be judged as independent from any broad contemporary stylistic movement.

By drawing inspiration from many sources and combining them to form a symbolic and highly individual design vocabulary, Mackintosh can be seen to have developed his own style. In this regard, one of the major influences on the symbolic content of his work was the ancient tradition of Celtic art, and this can be particularly recognized in his early watercolours such as *The Tree of Personal Effort* (ill. p. 162) and *The Tree of Influence* (ill. p. 162). Mackintosh identified with the Celts' pagan reverence for the natural world. The Celts were a pantheistic people who evolved a cult of tree personification and individuals were accorded the attributes of trees— the oak, for example, signified strength. Central to Celtic mythology was the "Craobh an Eolais" or "Tree of Knowledge", a vital link between the human world and the world inhabited by deities. Mackintosh returned to this theme time and again, perhaps most notably in the carved decoration of the pulpit at Queen's Cross Church.

The impact of Japanese culture was also strongly felt in Glasgow. In parallel to developments in French Post-Impressionism, "The Glasgow Boys" —a group of avant-garde painters that included among others Edward Atkinson Hornel (1864–1933) and George Henry (1858–1943)[10]—were working in a style which drew much of its inspiration from Japanese art. As a prominent member of the Glasgow art set, Mackintosh would have had first-hand knowledge of their work and would also have been aware of work by members of the Aesthetic Movement, such as Edward William Godwin (1833–1886) and the painter James Abbott McNeill Whistler (1834–1903). The Aesthetic Movement, an ornamentally driven Anglo-Oriental style, ran counter to the Arts & Crafts Movement and was exemplified by the writings and decadent lifestyle of Oscar Wilde (1854–1900) as well as the later graphic work of Aubrey Beardsley (1872–1898). Given the love of all things Japanese in the later nineteenth century, it is not surprising that the Glasgow Corporation held an exhibition of Japanese and Persian decorative art in 1882. At this event, the Glasgow-born designer Christopher Dresser (1834–1904) gave several lectures on the art of Japan, and—although 14 years old at the time—it is inconceivable that Mackintosh did not later feel their impact.

Mackintosh regarded the art and design of Japan as a historically unencumbered source of inspiration, and its influence is apparent in many of the forms and motifs that he adopted. In particular, Mackintosh incorporated in his interiors a modified version of the Japanese structural style of *Sinkabe Kozo* by using screens and painted wooden elements to create spatial divisions. Perhaps even more directly, as has been suggested by Hiroaki Kimura,

Poster for *The Scottish Musical Review*, colour lithograph, 1896
Plakat für *The Scottish Musical Review*, Farblithographie
Affiche pour *The Scottish Musical Review*, lithographie en couleur
53.3 x 40 cm

eines Interieurs an als auf virtuoses handwerkliches Können und eine Überbetonung des Funktionalen. In erster Linie ging es ihm um den ästhetischen Gesamteindruck, weniger um die technischen Mittel, mit denen dieses Ziel erreicht werden sollte. Deshalb hatte Mackintosh nur eine lose Verbindung zur Arts-and-Crafts-Bewegung. Obwohl er zu denen gehörte, die einen wesentlichen Einfluß auf den Jugendstil ausübten, stimmte er auch mit diesem nicht vorbehaltlos überein, denn er mißbilligte die Verwendung des Ornaments für rein dekorative Zwecke. Er war ein vollkommen eigenständiger Designer und muß unabhängig von jeder zeitgenössischen Stilrichtung gesehen werden.

Mackintosh entwickelte seinen persönlichen Stil, indem er Inspirationen aus vielen Quellen bezog und sie zu einer symbolischen, ganz individuellen Formensprache verband. Die uralte Tradition keltischer Kunst beeinflußte ihn besonders stark, wie sich insbesondere an seinen frühen Aquarellen, z.B. *The Tree of Personal Effort* (Der Baum der persönlichen Anstrengung; Abb. S. 162) und *The Tree of Influence* (Der Baum des Einflusses; Abb. S. 162), erkennen läßt. Mackintosh identifizierte sich mit der heidnischen Naturverehrung der Kelten, die Menschen die Eigenschaften von Bäumen zuschrieb, z.B. die Kraft der Eiche. Im Mittelpunkt der keltischen Mythologie stand „The Craobh an Eolais" (Der Baum der Erkenntnis), ein lebenswichtiges Bindeglied zwischen der Menschen- und der Götterwelt. Mackintosh kehrte immer wieder zu diesem Thema zurück, vielleicht besonders eindrucksvoll im Schnitzdekor der Kanzel der Queen's Cross Church.

Auch in Glasgow fand die japanische Kultur ihren künstlerischen Niederschlag: Parallel zu den Entwicklungen im französischen Nachimpressionismus arbeiteten die „Glasgow Boys"—eine Gruppe von Avantgarde-Malern, zu denen unter anderem Edward Atkinson Hornel (1864–1933) und George Henry (1858–1943)[10] gehörten—in einem an der japanischen Kunst orientierten Stil. Es ist anzunehmen, daß Mackintosh als prominentes Mitglied der Glasgower Kunstszene ihre Arbeit aus erster Hand kannte und ihm auch das Schaffen von Mitgliedern des Aesthetic Movement (der Ästhetik-Bewegung), wie Edward William Godwin (1833–1886) und der Maler James Abbott McNeill Whistler (1834–1903), vertraut war. Dieser Ästhetizismus, eine vom Ornamentalen ausgehende anglo-asiatische Stilrichtung, die in der Dichtung und dem dekadenten Lebensstil Oscar Wildes (1854–1900) und den späten Zeichnungen Aubrey Beardsleys (1872–1898) ihren Ausdruck fand, stand im Gegensatz zur Arts-and-Crafts-Bewegung. Angesichts der Begeisterung für alles Japanische im späten 19. Jahrhundert ist es nicht verwunderlich, daß die Glasgow Corporation 1882 eine japanische und persische Kunstgewerbeausstellung organisierte. Im Rahmen dieser Veranstal-

«Arbre de la Connaissance», qui reliait le monde des hommes à celui des dieux. Mackintosh utilisa ce thème à plusieurs reprises, et en particulier dans les décorations sculptées de la chaire de la Queen's Cross Church.

Le japonisme eut son heure de gloire à Glasgow grâce aux relations économiques privilégiées qu'entrenait cette ville avec le Japon. A la même époque que les post-impressionnistes en France, un groupe de peintres d'avant-garde, les «Glasgow Boys», dont Edward Atkinson Hornel (1864–1933) et George Henry (1858–1943)[10], travaillaient dans un style fortement inspiré de l'art japonais. Personnalité du petit monde artistique de Glasgow, Mackintosh connaissait sans doute fort bien leur travail. Il n'ignorait pas non plus la production du Mouvement Esthétique ou de «l'Art pour l'Art», représenté par Edward William Godwin (1833–1886) et le peintre James Abbott McNeill Whistler (1834–1903). Le Mouvement Esthétique, style décoratif anglais aux connotations orientalistes, s'opposait aux Arts & Crafts. On le connaît par les écrits et par le style de vie «décadent» d'Oscar Wilde (1854–1900) et par les œuvres graphiques d'Aubrey Beardsley (1872–1898). Cet engouement pour l'art japonais à la fin du XIXème siècle explique que la Glasgow Corporation (la municipalité) ait organisé une exposition d'art décoratif japonais et persan en 1882. A cette occasion un décorateur né à Glasgow, Christopher Dresser (1834–1904), donna une série de conférences sur l'art japonais. Mackintosh n'avait que 14 ans à l'époque, mais il est vraisemblable qu'il a été marqué par cet événement.

Mackintosh voyait dans l'art et le design japonais une source d'inspiration historiquement vierge. L'influence japonaise est évidente dans toute son œuvre. Il introduisit plus particulièrement dans ses intérieurs une version remaniée du style de partition dit *Sinkabe Kozo*, en utilisant des écrans et des éléments de bois peint pour diviser l'espace. De façon plus littérale encore, les curieux motifs de la grille en fer forgé de la façade nord de la School of Art (ill. p. 52) sont inspirés des emblèmes héraldiques japonais Mon[11], comme le fait observer Hiroaki Kimura. Les qualités fonctionnelles de l'architecture japonaise et de son espace fluide ne pouvaient manquer de plaire à Mackintosh. On verra d'ailleurs que beaucoup de ses projets sont non seulement unifiés sur le plan fonctionnel, mais qu'ils atteignent aussi à la paix et à l'harmonie spirituelle par leur pureté et leur équilibre.

LES GLASGOW FOUR

Alors qu'il était étudiant à la School of Art de Glasgow, Mackintosh se lia d'amitié avec J. Herbert MacNair (1868–1955), apprenti comme lui à l'agence Honeyman & Keppie. Il cherchait, lui aussi, à élaborer un nouvel idiome visuel symboliste. Les deux

Poster for *The Scottish Musical Review*, colour lithograph, 1896
Plakat für *The Scottish Musical Review*, Farblithographie
Affiche pour *The Scottish Musical Review*, lithographie en couleur
230 x 85.8 cm

the curious motifs used on the iron screen of the Glasgow School of Art's north façade (ill. p. 52) are highly characteristic of Japanese heraldic emblems or *Mon*.[11] Certainly the functional qualities of open-plan Japanese architecture appealed to Mackintosh, and many of his projects were not only function-ally unified, but achieve tranquillity and spiritual harmony through purity and balance.

THE GLASGOW FOUR

Frances Macdonald:
Candlestick, c. 1896
Kerzenleuchter
Chandelier

While studying at the Glasgow School of Art, Mack-intosh became good friends with J. Herbert Mac-Nair (1868–1955), a fellow apprentice at Honeyman & Keppie. Like Mackintosh, he too was attempting to evolve a new visual and symbolic language in design. With this shared objective they worked closely together and were eventually introduced by Francis H. "Fra" Newbery (1853–1946), the head of the School of Art, to two English sisters of Scottish descent, Frances (1873–1921) and Margaret (1864–1933) Macdonald, who had enrolled at the School of Art in 1891 as painting day students. Newbery, in identifying the similarities between their work and that of Mackintosh and MacNair, suggested they form a close working collaboration.

Exhibiting together for the first time in Liège in 1895, "The Glasgow Four", as they quickly became known, possessed a readily identifiable style that was influenced by the eastern eroticism and sinuous line of Aubrey Beardsley's illustrations in *The Yellow Book*. The content of their work was inspired by Continental symbolism, such as that of the Paris based illustrator, Carlos Schwabe (1866–1926), and the painter of Indo-Dutch descent, Jan Toorop (1858–1928), whose work was inhabited by melan-cholic ethereal spirits. The work of both these artists was published in *The Studio* in 1897[12] and al-most certainly would have been seen by The Four.

The Four's work also drew inspiration from the Pre-Raphaelite Brotherhood's sentimental and nos-talgic return to medievalism which announced a desire to "escape from the present into a world of beautiful regrets"[13]. William Gaunt wrote in his book *The Pre-Raphaelite Dream* that the Brotherhood "looked on an age materialist in essence and gov-erned by machinery as one that could not be accep-ted (...) they lived therefore a life of the imagination and nourished it from sources outside the material-ism that surrounded them (...) A special creation of Victorianism was anti-Victorianism"[14]. The Four's quest for a symbolic language that would infuse their work with spiritual and mystical content was borne out of similar sentiments and, like the work of the Brotherhood, can be seen as a rejection of the conservatism and materialism of the Victorian age.

After the relative success of the Liège exhibition, The Four were invited to participate in the Arts & Crafts Society Exhibition of 1896 in London. Their

tung hielt der aus Glasgow stammende Designer Christopher Dresser (1834–1904) mehrere Vorträge über japanische Kunst, und obgleich Mackintosh zu diesem Zeitpunkt erst 14 Jahre alt war, ist es kaum vorstellbar, daß er nicht später von dieser Ausstel-lung beeinflußt wurde.

Mackintosh betrachtete japanische Kunst als eine historisch unbelastete Quelle der Inspiration. Ihr Einfluß wird in vielen Formen und Motiven, die er verwendete, deutlich. Vor allem bezog er eine abge-wandelte Version des Stils von *Sinkabe Kozo* in seine Innenausstattungen ein, indem er Trennwände und bemalte Holzelemente für die Raumaufteilung nutz-te. Vielleicht—darauf hat Hiroaki Kimura hinge-wiesen—zeigt sich dieser Einfluß noch deutlicher in den seltsamen Motiven am schmiedeeisernen Gitterwerk der Nordfassade der Glasgow School of Art (Abb. S. 52), die typisch für japanische Wappen-emblemata, sogenannte *Mon*[11]-Schilde, sind. Zwei-fellos gefiel Mackintosh der funktionale Charakter der offen angelegten japanischen Architektur. Viele seiner Entwürfe zeichnen sich nicht nur durch Ein-heitlichkeit in der Funktion aus, sie vermitteln dar-über hinaus durch ihre Klarheit und Ausgewogen-heit Ruhe und geistige Harmonie.

DIE GLASGOW FOUR

Während seines Studiums an der Glasgow School of Art freundete sich Mackintosh mit J. Herbert MacNair (1868–1955) an, der ebenfalls als Zeichner im Architekturbüro Honeyman & Keppie angestellt war. Wie Mackintosh versuchte auch er, eine neue symbolische Formensprache zu entwickeln. Francis H. „Fra" Newbery (1853–1946), der Direktor der Glasgow School of Art, machte die Freunde mit Frances (1873–1921) und Margaret (1864–1933) Mac-donald, zwei englischen Schwestern schottischer Herkunft, bekannt, die ab ca. 1891 Malkurse an der Glasgow School of Art belegt hatten. Newbery, der die Gemeinsamkeiten zwischen Macdonalds, Mac-Nairs und Mackintoshs künstlerischen Bestrebun-gen erkannt hatte, legte ihnen nahe, sich zu einer Arbeitsgemeinschaft zusammenzuschließen.

Die Glasgow Four, wie sie bald genannt wurden, stellten 1895 zum ersten Mal gemeinsam in Lüttich aus. Sie hatten einen charakteristischen Stil, der von der fernöstlichen Erotik und der geschwunge-nen Linie der Illustrationen Aubrey Beardsleys in *The Yellow Book* inspiriert wurde. Inhaltlich empfin-gen sie Impulse vom europäischen Symbolismus, so von dem in Paris ansässigen Zeichner Carlos Schwabe (1866–1926) und dem indisch-niederlän-dischen Maler Jan Toorop (1858–1928), dessen Werk melancholische Geister bevölkern. Die Vier haben mit großer Wahrscheinlichkeit die 1897 in *The Studio*[12] veröffentlichten Arbeiten dieser beiden Künstler gekannt.

In ihrem geistigen und mystischen Gehalt bezog

amis travaillaient en commun. C'est alors que Francis H. «Fra» Newbery (1853–1946), directeur de l'école, les présenta à deux sœurs anglaises d'origine écossaise, Frances (1873–1921) et Margaret Macdonald (1864–1933). Elles s'étaient inscrites à la Glasgow School of Art en 1891 pour y suivre des cours de peinture pendant la journée. Sensible aux affinités entre le travail des sœurs et celui de Mackintosh et MacNair, Newbery les engagea à travailler en étroite collaboration.

On les appela rapidement les «Glasgow Four» (les Quatre de Glasgow). Leur première exposition commune eut lieu à Liège en 1895. Leur style caractéristique était influencé par la réinterprétation que faisait Beardsley des estampes érotiques japonaises et de leurs lignes sinueuses dans ses illustrations du *Yellow Book*. Quant au contenu, il s'inspirait ouvertement du symbolisme européen: par exemple celui de l'illustrateur Carlos Schwabe (1866–1926) qui vivait à Paris, ou du peintre métis néerlandais Jan Toorop (1858–1928), qui représentait surtout des esprits mélancoliques et éthérés. Le travail de ces deux artistes ayant été publié par *The Studio* en 1897[12], il est quasiment certain que les Quatre en ont eu connaissance.

Le contenu spirituel et mystique de leur œuvre s'inspirait également de la «Fraternité» préraphaélite. Cette nostalgie romantique du Moyen-Age révélait un désir «d'échapper au présent pour vivre dans un monde de regrets magnifiques»[13]. Dans *The Pre-Raphaelite Dream*, William Gaunt dit de la «Fraternité» préraphaélite qu'elle considérait «son époque comme intrinsèquement matérialiste, soumise à la machine, et inacceptable en tant que telle (…) Les préraphaélites menaient donc une vie imaginaire et la nourrissaient à des sources extérieures au matérialisme qui les entourait. (…) Une forme spécifiquement victorienne de l'anti-victorianisme»[14]. Des idéaux similaires animaient les Quatre de Glasgow dans leur recherche d'un langage symbolique qui saurait donner à leur œuvre un contenu spirituel. Au même titre que les préraphaélites, ils rejetaient le conservatisme et le matérialisme de l'ère victorienne.

Après leur succès d'estime à l'Exposition de Liège, les Quatre furent invités à participer à l'Exposition de la Arts & Crafts Society à Londres en 1896. Leur contribution surprenante suscita les railleries du public et de la critique. Un journaliste alla jusqu'à écrire que leur travail était «le résultat de l'enthousiasme juvénile» et «se complaisait dans la laideur absolue»[15]. Seul Gleeson White, rédacteur en chef de *The Studio*, semble avoir apprécié, bien que timidement, la contribution des Ecossais: «Si ces artistes ne deviennent un jour chefs de file de leur propre école, alors nous nous serons totalement fourvoyés. Il est probable que ceux qui se moquent d'eux aujourd'hui seront les premiers à les porter au pinacle demain.»[16]

Margaret Macdonald:
Summer, design for a stained-glass window, c. 1894
Sommer, Entwurf für eine Bleiverglasung
Eté, projet de vitrail
51.7 x 21.8 cm

& Keppie, as Mackintosh had been previously en-
gaged to John Keppie's sister, Jessie. Two years prior
to John Honeyman's retirement in 1904, Mackintosh
was nonetheless made a partner in the firm, but his
relationship with Keppie, which had hitherto been
quite close, rapidly declined.

Early in his career, prior to his promotion to
partner at Honeyman & Keppie, Mackintosh co-
designed a number of buildings, including the Glasgow Herald building (ill. pp. 46–47) from 1893 to
1894, followed by Queen Margaret's Medical College
from 1894 to 1896 and the Martyrs' Public School
(ill. pp. 48–49) in 1895. Conceived under the aus-
pices of the firm, these projects reflect the somewhat compromising stylistic preferences of his em-
ployers and little of Mackintosh's individual style is
readily apparent. It was not until the competition
for the design of the new Glasgow School of Art
(ill. pp. 52–63) in 1896 that he was allowed a greater
freedom of expression. On winning this brief, Mackintosh's stature as a progressive architect in his own
right was firmly established.

The Glasgow School of Art, built in two phases,
and finally completed in 1909, is rightly referred
to as "Mackintosh's masterwork". Thomas Howarth
has described it as "a building designed primarily
to fulfil its purpose well, with, of course some artist's
license, for the time of the functionalist pure and
simple had not yet come. It was and it remains
Mackintosh's most representative work, and it is
undoubtedly his most important contribution to
the new movement."[28] With this project Mackintosh
was able to give three-dimensional realization to his
firmly held architectural ideals. The School of Art
represents a harmonic synthesis of the traditional
and the modern, the beautiful and the utilitarian,
the national and the international. It is this balancing of opposites combined with Mackintosh's
considered use of symbolic decoration that fosters
a spiritual connection with his work and renders
the School of Art such an enduringly successful
building.

Mackintosh also believed that the quality of mass
in a building was essential to its success, and wrote
in an untitled paper on architecture of 1892, "I think
you will admit that it is the want of bulk which is
the chief blemish of modern street architecture (...)
the eye is distressed at the huge lofty tenements
resting to all appearance on nothing more stable
than glass for the real actual supports are easily
overlooked. (...) These two comparatively modern
materials, iron and glass, though eminently suitable
for many purposes will never worthily take the place
of stone because of this defect—the want of mass."
Referring to the Modern Movement's preference for
these two materials and the potential they allow for
reducing visible structure in large buildings, he
continued: "Time has passed, and practical experience has shown that apart altogether from any

eng zusammen; viele Projekte, die allein Charles
zugeschrieben werden, sind wohl das Resultat ge-
meinsamer Arbeit, obwohl dies trotz Margarets un-
bezweifelbarer Begabung als Malerin nur selten an-
erkannt wird. Ihre Zusammenarbeit kommentierte
Mackintosh mit den Worten: „Margaret ist ein Genie, ich habe nur Talent", und 1927 erinnerte er sie
daran mit den Worten: „(...) du bist die Hälfte, wenn
nicht zwei Drittel bei all meinen architektonischen
Bemühungen gewesen."[27]

Margaret—zum Zeitpunkt ihrer Heirat sechsund-
dreißig (vier Jahre älter als Charles)—war eine
emanzipierte Frau mit kastanienbraunen Haaren,
die ihren Mann im Auf und Ab seines Lebens un-
ablässig unterstützte. Sie waren Seelengefährten,
die während ihrer achtundzwanzigjährigen Ehe
eine stete Zuneigung zueinander empfanden. Obwohl sie allen Berichten zufolge Kinder sehr gern
hatten, blieb die Ehe kinderlos. Ihre Verbindung
wird das Arbeitsklima bei Honeyman & Keppie
nicht gerade günstig beeinflußt haben, da Mackintosh vorher mit John Keppies Schwester Jessie
verlobt gewesen war. Trotzdem wurde Mackintosh
zwei Jahre vor John Honeymans Ausscheiden aus
dem Geschäft (1904) Teilhaber der Firma; seine bis
dahin enge Beziehung zu Keppie verschlechterte
sich freilich zusehends.

Schon zu Beginn seiner Laufbahn, noch vor seinem Aufstieg zum Teilhaber von Honeyman & Keppie, entwarf Mackintosh mehrere Gebäude, so 1893
bis 1894 den Erweiterungsbau des Glasgow Herald
(Abb. S. 46–47), von 1894 bis 1896 das Queen Margaret's Medical College und 1895 die Martyrs' Public
School (Abb. S. 48–49). Diese Projekte spiegeln die
eher konservativen Stilvorstellungen seiner Arbeit-
geber und zeigen auf den ersten Blick nur wenig
von Mackintoshs eigener Handschrift. Erst die Aus-
schreibung für den Neubau der Glasgow School of
Art 1896 (Abb. S. 52–63) gewährte ihm eine größere
Ausdrucksfreiheit. Mit diesem Auftrag, der zwar der
Firma zugesprochen wurde, den Mackintosh aber
selbständig ausführte, begründete er seinen Ruf als
progressiver eigenständiger Architekt.

Der in zwei Phasen errichtete und 1909 schließlich vollendete Bau der Glasgow School of Art wird
mit Recht als „Mackintoshs Meisterwerk" bezeichnet. Thomas Howarth hat es als ein Gebäude be-
schrieben, „das in erster Linie seinen Zweck erfüllen
sollte, wenn auch mit gewisser künstlerischer Freiheit, denn die Zeit des rein Funktionalen und Einfachen war noch nicht gekommen. Es war und bleibt
Mackintoshs repräsentativstes Werk, und es ist zweifellos sein bedeutendster Beitrag zur neuen Bewegung."[28] Mit diesem Projekt gab Mackintosh seinen
Architekturidealen eine dreidimensionale Gestalt.
Die Glasgow School of Art ist eine harmonische
Synthese von Traditionellem und Modernem, Schö-
nem und Nützlichem, Nationalem und Internationa-
lem. Dieser Ausgleich von Gegensätzen, verbunden

Thomas Howarth en fait la description suivante:
«C'est un bâtiment d'abord conçu pour remplir une
fonction, avec bien sûr quelques libertés que s'est
autorisé l'artiste. L'époque n'était pas encore au
fonctionnalisme pur et dur. Elle reste l'œuvre la plus
personnelle de Mackintosh, et sa contribution la
plus importante au nouveau mouvement architectural.»[28] Avec cette école, Mackintosh a pu traduire
dans l'espace ses convictions en matière d'architecture. La School of Art représente une synthèse har-
monieuse entre la tradition et la modernité, le beau
et l'utile, le national et l'international. C'est cet
équilibre entre les extrêmes, auquel vient s'ajouter
l'utilisation mesurée d'ornements d'esprit symboliste, qui fait la force spirituelle de l'œuvre et qui
lui donne aujourd'hui encore toute sa prégnance.

Mackintosh pensait aussi que la qualité des masses était essentielle pour la réussite d'une construction. C'est ce qu'il écrivait dans un essai sans titre
daté de 1892: «Vous reconnaîtrez comme moi que le
plus grand défaut de l'architecture urbaine aujourd'hui est son absence de masse (...) On éprouve
une sensation de malaise à voir tous ces grands immeubles de rapport qui donnent l'impression de ne
reposer que sur du verre, tant les points porteurs
sont peu visibles (...) Ces deux matériaux relativement modernes, le fer et le verre, si commodes qu'ils
soient, ne remplaceront jamais valablement la
pierre à cause de ce défaut, l'absence de masse.»
Toujours à propos de la prédilection du mouvement
moderne pour ces matériaux et pour leur capacité
à restreindre la structure visible des grands bâtiments, il poursuit: «Le temps et l'expérience ont
montré que le fer et le verre, même s'ils possèdent
les qualités requises de stabilité et de confort, man-
quent à ce point de l'apparence de la stabilité, qu'ils
ne pourront jamais susciter un style propre en architecture domestique, civile ou religieuse.»[29] Il
concluait que l'architecture devait être conçue pour
l'esprit autant que pour le corps. Les cercles et les
carrés qui reviennent constamment dans la Glasgow
School of Art symbolisent respectivement le corps
et l'esprit d'après Carl Gustav Jung (1875–1961),
dont Mackintosh avait étudié les écrits. Il croyait
aussi que l'expression de la beauté était aussi importante que la fonction physique d'un bâtiment, que
l'utilité ne pouvait être un but en soi et ne pouvait
se justifier en dehors du contexte. Mackintosh conçut pour la School of Art un mobilier robuste aux
formes simples destiné aux parties communes du
bâtiment. Il intégra des sièges encastrés dans les
couloirs pour les étudiants. Il dessina aussi des
meubles plus raffinés et légers pour les salles réser-
vées au corps enseignant, bureau du directeur et
salle du conseil par exemple (ill. p. 60–61).

Les projets de salons de thé de Mackintosh pour
l'énergique Miss Cranston avaient la même ambition
fonctionnelle et sociale que ses autres bâtiments
publics. Dès les années 1870, le mouvement anti-

Margaret Macdonald-Mackintosh, Charles Rennie Mackintosh, c. 1900

Margaret Macdonald-Mackintosh, c. 1900

defect in stability or actual comfort the want of appearance of stability is fatal to the introduction of such a style for either domestic, civil, or ecclesiastical buildings."[29] In this paper, Mackintosh concluded that architecture must be constructed for the mind as well as the body. The circular and square forms that can be found repeated throughout the School of Art symbolize—according to Carl Gustav Jung (1875–1961), whose writings Mackintosh had studied—the body and the spirit respectively. Mackintosh also believed that the expression of beauty was of equal importance to a building's physical function and that utility alone could only be selfishly realised and would not be wholly justified if it did not consider the context of its environment.

For the School of Art, Mackintosh designed sturdy furniture with simple forms for the common areas of the building and incorporated in the scheme built-in settles in the corridors for the students to use while socializing. In contrast to the solidly built utility furniture of the common parts, Mackintosh created more refined and visually light furniture for the quarters used by the teaching staff, such as the director's room and the boardroom (ill. pp. 60–61).

Catherine Cranston, c. 1900

Mackintosh's tea room designs for the individualistic proprietress Miss Catherine Cranston were as appropriate for their usage as any of his other public buildings and just as socially motivated. Commercial tea rooms had been opened as early as the 1870s, as part of the Temperance Movement in Glasgow, in an attempt to alleviate the surge in daytime drunkenness amongst the city's workers. Not only did the tea rooms have to function well as catering establishments, they had to be elegant, refined and above all novel, so as to attract business away from the public houses. They quickly became fashionable, appealing to both men and women, and even often functioned as art galleries where work by contemporary artists such as the Glasgow Boys could be publicly exhibited.

In 1884, Catherine Cranston opened her first tea room, having convinced her reluctant father to help her with the venture. Fortunately, the business flourished and it was not long before she came up with the novel idea of a restaurant-cum-tea room that had the added attraction of billiard tables and smoking rooms. In 1892, her concept was realized when her husband, Major John Cochrane, purchased as a wedding present the whole of the property she already partly occupied, 114 Argyle Street. Bolstered by the success of this business, in 1895 she took possession of two further premises at 205–209 Ingram Street and 91–93 Buchanan Street and, in 1903, additionally acquired the Willow Tea Rooms site in Sauchiehall Street.

From 1896 to 1917, Mackintosh's skills were variously employed in all four tea rooms, from the design of small elements in a larger scheme, as at Buchanan Street (ill. pp. 50–51), to the design of a

mit Mackintoshs besonnenem Gebrauch symbolischer Dekorelemente ist es letztlich, der einen geistigen Bezug zu seiner Arbeit ermöglicht und der Architektur der Glasgow School of Art eine so dauerhafte Bedeutung beschert.

In einem 1892 verfaßten Aufsatz zur Architektur äußerte sich Mackintosh zum Problem der Masse, das er für wesentlich für die Wirkung eines Bauwerks hielt. Der Mangel an Masse sei der Hauptfehler moderner Straßenarchitektur, da die riesigen, hohen Mietshäuser, die allem Anschein nach lediglich auf Glas als einzig sicherem Halt ruhten, den Betrachter beunruhigten, weil die tatsächlichen Stützen leicht übersehen würden. Die beiden vergleichsweise modernen Baustoffe Eisen und Glas, die sich für viele Zwecke hervorragend eigneten, könnten wegen des Mangels an Masse die Schwere des Steins nicht wirklich ersetzen. Die praktische Erfahrung habe inzwischen gezeigt, daß ganz abgesehen von Schwächen bei der Stabilität oder Nachteilen in der Bequemlichkeit der Anschein mangelnder Festigkeit verhängnisvoll für Wohnhäuser, Verwaltungsgebäude oder kirchliche Bauwerke sei.[29] Mackintosh kam in dieser Abhandlung zu dem Schluß, daß Architektur gleichermaßen den Geist wie den Körper berücksichtigen müsse. Die Kurven und quadratischen Formen, die sich im ganzen Komplex der Glasgow School of Art finden lassen, versinnbildlichen nach Carl Gustav Jung (1875–1961), mit dessen Schriften sich Mackintosh eingehend beschäftigt hatte, jeweils Leib und Seele. Zudem war Mackintosh der Überzeugung, daß der Ausdruck von Schönheit ebenso bedeutend sei wie die physikalische Funktion eines Gebäudes. Nützlichkeit allein ließe sich ohne Berücksichtigung der Umgebung nicht rechtfertigen.

Für die Gemeinschaftsbereiche der Glasgow School of Art entwarf Mackintosh ein stabiles Mobiliar in einfachen Formen, auf den Korridoren gab es Bänke, um die Kommunikation zwischen den Studenten zu fördern. Im Gegensatz zu den Gebrauchsmöbeln der Gemeinschaftsräume schuf Mackintosh für die Räume des Lehrpersonals, des Direktors und den Konferenzsaal eine elegantere, optisch leicht wirkende Inneneinrichtung (Abb. S. 60–61).

Bei der Gestaltung der Teesalons für die eigenwilligen Miss Catherine Cranston ließ sich Mackintosh ebenso wie bei seinen öffentlichen Gebäuden vom Prinzip der Funktionalität und sozialen Gedanken leiten. Teestuben gab es in Glasgow schon seit den siebziger Jahren. Sie waren Teil der Glasgower Abstinenzbewegung und dienten dem Ziel, den steigenden Alkoholkonsum der Arbeiter einzudämmen. Die Teesalons sollten nicht nur Speisen und Getränke anbieten, sondern auch elegant, kultiviert und ungewöhnlich sein, um so Kunden von den Pubs wegzulocken. Wegen ihrer Anziehungskraft sowohl auf Männer als auch auf Frauen kamen sie rasch in Mode und wurden oft für öffentliche

alcoolique avait suscité l'ouverture de salons de thé qui entendaient détourner les travailleurs des pubs où ils s'enivraient consciencieusement à toute heure du jour. Ces établissements devaient être irréprochables sur le plan du service; ils devaient aussi être élégants, raffinés et surtout assez originaux pour attirer la clientèle habituelle des débits de boissons. Ils devinrent très vite à la mode, s'adressant aussi bien aux hommes qu'aux femmes et jouant parfois le rôle de galerie d'art où des artistes contemporains pouvaient exposer leurs œuvres.

En 1884, avec l'aide financière de son père, Miss Cranston ouvrit son premier salon de thé au 114 Argyle Street. Le succès fut presque immédiat, et elle ne tarda pas à imaginer le nouveau concept d'un restaurant-salon-de-thé, auquel s'ajoutaient une salle de billard et un fumoir. Elle put le réaliser en 1895, lorsque son mari, le Major Cochrane, lui offrit en cadeau de mariage la totalité de l'immeuble du 114, qu'elle n'occupait jusque-là que partiellement. Encouragée par son succès, elle acheta en 1895 deux nouveaux locaux au 205–209 Ingram Street et au 91–93 Buchanan Street. En 1903, elle fit aussi l'acquisition du local de Sauchiehall Street, qui allait devenir le Willow Tea Rooms.

De 1896 à 1917, Mackintosh travailla comme architecte, designer et décorateur dans ces quatre salons de thé: de la conception d'éléments de détail pour un ensemble comme à Buchanan Street (ill. p. 50–51) jusqu'à la conception totale du bâtiment, mobilier et décoration compris, comme au Willow Tea Rooms (ill. p. 112–121). Il disposait d'un budget moins limité que pour ses bâtiments publics. Les contraintes stylistiques étaient également moindres que dans ses commandes de villas. Cette liberté permit à Mackintosh de créer ses meubles les plus célèbres. C'est pour Argyle Street qu'il a conçu la célèbre chaise à haut dossier avec la découpe ovale (ill. p. 67); et c'est pour les Willow Tea Rooms qu'il a dessiné sa chaise à dossier courbe en petits bois et la chaise-échelle mondialement connue (ill. p. 117).

Catherine Cranston laissait presque totalement carte blanche à son designer. Mais de tels clients sont rares, et Mackintosh ne devait jamais retrouver la même autonomie de création. L'ironie du sort veut que ce soit justement lui, grand alcoolique devant l'Eternel, qui ait dessiné ces temples de l'abstinence qu'étaient les salons de thé de Miss Cranston.

En mettant la beauté au même rang que la fonction, Mackintosh a fait la transition entre le XIXème et le XXème siècle dans le domaine de l'architecture et du design. Il pensait que la créativité et l'invention comptaient plus que le simple talent graphique. Il avait pris comme devise une citation de J. D. Sedding: «Il y a davantage d'espoir dans l'erreur sincère que dans la perfection glacée du virtuose.» Il l'a intégrée, en anglais et en allemand, dans des œuvres graphiques qui se trouvent actuellement à la Hunterian Art Gallery de Glasgow.

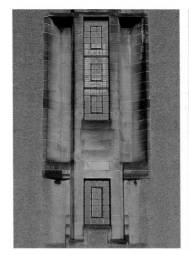

Glasgow School of Art, details of the façades
Fassadendetails der Glasgow School of Art
Détails des façades de la Glasgow School of Art

complete and wholly unified building such as the Willow Tea Rooms (ill. pp. 112–121). The briefs for these projects were not as financially constrained as his public buildings nor as stylistically restricted as his domestic commissions. This freedom to work expressively gave rise to some of Mackintosh's best known furniture designs; for Argyle Street he designed his famous high-backed chair with pierced oval splat (ill. p. 67), while for the Willow Tea Rooms he designed his novel curved lattice-back chair and his ubiquitous ladder-back chair (ill. p. 117).

Catherine Cranston was an exceptional client who virtually granted Mackintosh a creative and financial *carte blanche*. Sadly, patrons like this were rare and Mackintosh was never again to experience the same professional autonomy. Having been so involved in the promotion and success of these establishments dedicated to the cause of abstinence, it is deeply ironic that Mackintosh almost certainly suffered from a personal addiction to alcohol.

In stressing the importance of beauty as well as function, Mackintosh bridged the gap between 19th and 20th century theories in architecture and design. He believed that creativity and inventiveness were more important than a talent for representation, stating: "There is hope in honest error; none in the icy perfection of the mere stylist." Mackintosh used this John D. Sedding quotation as his own motto and designed a graphic work which incorporated it—he also translated it into German for another work. These "drawings" are now in the collection of the Hunterian Art Gallery, Glasgow.

While thoroughly committed to much of the philosophy of the early Modern Movement, Mackintosh was also rooted in the architectural practices of an earlier age; he did not like to concern himself with the practical considerations of drawing up time schedules, costings and working to a tight budget. His refusal or inability to work within his clients' constraints, however, was not so much due to a lack of competence as it was to his own underlying character flaws and the pressures of professional practice. Mackintosh's obstinacy, which must be seen as symptomatic of his compulsive psyche, cost him dearly later on in his career.

The construction and detailing of Hill House (ill. pp. 102–111) exemplifies Mackintosh's single-minded pursuit of a perfectly unified architectural design. Prior to designing this project, Mackintosh insisted on spending a weekend at the Dunblane home of his client (the publisher, Walter Blackie) so as to understand how the family operated domestically. At their first meeting in 1902, Blackie mentioned to Mackintosh that he "fancied" grey harling and a slate roof, both traditional Scottish materials. The latter request, however, was to become something of a problem, for while Hill House was being built the Ballachulish slate quarries went on strike. To Blackie's increasing frustration, Mackintosh refused to

High-backed chair with coloured glass insets, designed for the Room de Luxe, Willow Tea Rooms

Stuhl mit hoher Rückenlehne und farbigen Glaseinlagen, entworfen für den „Room de Luxe" in den Willow Tea Rooms

Chaise à haut dossier incrustée de verre, conçue pour le «Room de Luxe», Willow Tea Rooms

Ausstellungen zeitgenössischer Künstler wie der Glasgow Boys genutzt.

1884 eröffnete Catherine Cranston ihren ersten Teesalon in der Argyle Street 114, nachdem sie ihren widerstrebenden Vater überzeugt hatte, sie dabei finanziell zu unterstützen. Glücklicherweise florierte das Geschäft, und sie kam bald auf die Idee, die Teestube mit einem Restaurant zu kombinieren und zusätzlich mit Billardtischen und Rauchzimmern auszustatten. 1892 konnte sie dieses Konzept verwirklichen, da ihr Mann, Major John Cochrane, ihr das ganze Haus in der Argyle Street 114 zur Hochzeit schenkte. Durch den Erfolg dieses Unternehmens ermutigt, übernahm sie zwei weitere Gebäude in der Ingram Street 205–209 und in der Buchanan Street 91–93; 1903 erwarb sie außerdem das Grundstück für die Willow Tea Rooms in der Sauchiehall Street.

Von 1896 bis 1917 verwandte Mackintosh sein Talent auf alle vier Teesalons—vom Entwurf von Details wie in der Buchanan Street (Abb. S. 50–51) bis zur gänzlichen Gestaltung von Gebäude, Mobiliar und Dekoration wie bei den Willow Tea Rooms (Abb. S. 112–121). Diese Projekte unterlagen weder den engen finanziellen Vorgaben seiner öffentlichen Bauten noch den stilistischen Einschränkungen anderer Privataufträge. Dieser künstlerischen Freiheit sind einige der bekanntesten Möbelentwürfe Mackintoshs zu verdanken. Für die Argyle Street schuf er seinen berühmten Stuhl mit der hohen Rückenlehne und dem ovalen, von einem Einschnitt durchbrochenen Kopfstück (Abb. S. 67); für die Willow Tea Rooms entwarf er seinen neuartigen Stuhl mit gebogener Gitterrückenlehne und den überall zu findenden Leiterrückenstuhl (Abb. S. 117).

Catherine Cranston war eine außergewöhnliche Kundin, die Mackintosh finanziell und künstlerisch fast unbeschränkte Vollmacht einräumte. Leider waren derart großzügige Auftraggeber selten, und Mackintosh hatte nie wieder Gelegenheit, so unabhängig zu arbeiten. Es mutet paradox an, daß Mackintosh, der höchstwahrscheinlich selber Alkoholiker war, sich so intensiv für die Förderung und den Erfolg dieser der Abstinenz gewidmeten Einrichtungen einsetzte.

Durch die Betonung sowohl der Schönheit als auch der Funktion überbrückte Mackintosh die Kluft zwischen den Architektur- und Designtheorien des 19. und 20. Jahrhunderts. Er war der Ansicht, daß schöpferische Kraft und Einfallsreichtum wichtiger seien als das Talent zur Darstellung. In diesem Sinne zitierte er John D. Sedding: „Der ehrliche Irrtum läßt hoffen, nicht aber die eisige Perfektion des bloßen Stilisten"—ein Zitat, das ihm als Motto diente und das er graphisch gestaltete, auch in deutscher Übersetzung. Diese „Schriftbilder" befinden sich heute in der Sammlung der Hunterian Art Gallery in Glasgow.

Obwohl Mackintosh sich der Philosophie der frühen Moderne zutiefst verpflichtet fühlte, blieb

Malgré tout le bien qu'il pensait du jeune Mouvement Moderne, Mackintosh restait attaché aux pratiques architecturales traditionnelles. Il ne se souciait guère de calendriers, de devis ou de contraintes financières. Son refus, ou son incapacité, de respecter les exigences des clients, tenait moins de l'incompétence que de son caractère difficile et des pressions inhérentes à la profession. Son obstination, qui traduit aussi sa fragilité psychologique, devait lui coûter cher par la suite.

La construction minutieuse de Hill House (ill. p. 102–111) montre bien l'acharnement que manifestait Mackintosh dans sa recherche de l'unité parfaite. Avant de commencer le projet, il voulut passer un week-end à Dunblane au domicile de son client, l'éditeur Walter Blackie, pour comprendre comment s'organisait la vie de famille. Dès leur première réunion en 1902, Blackie avait fait part à Mackintosh de son goût pour le *harling* gris (sorte de crépi rustique) et l'ardoise, matériaux écossais traditionnels. L'ardoise devait poser un problème pendant la construction de Hill House, car les ouvriers des carrières de Ballachulish se mirent en grève. Au grand dam de Blackie, Mackintosh refusa obstinément d'envisager un autre mode de couverture, et le chantier fut arrêté pendant six mois, jusqu'à ce que le conflit des carrières soit réglé.

L'intransigeance de Mackintosh n'allait pas sans poser des problèmes au commanditaire. Mais Blackie n'aurait jamais trouvé d'autre architecte qui puisse mieux satisfaire son exigence fondamentale, à savoir que «l'effet architectural doit provenir du regroupement des volumes plutôt que de la décoration surajoutée»[30]. L'agencement des pièces fut décidé avant la façade, ce qui fait sans doute de Hill House une des premières applications du slogan «La forme suit toujours la fonction». Mackintosh juxtaposa des éléments architecturaux traditionnels du style féodal, telle la tour-escalier et de grands murs nus, qui paraissent anticiper l'emploi du béton armé brut de décoffrage par le Mouvement Moderne. Il créa ainsi un bâtiment qui correspondait exactement aux critères fonctionnels et esthétiques de la commande.

De 1900, année de leur mariage, à 1906, les Mackintosh occupèrent un appartement-atelier au 120 Mains Street (ill. p. 72–75). Le côté vaste et aéré de leur salon était l'exacte antithèse des intérieurs édouardiens, encombrés par un mobilier massif et obscurcis par des couches de persiennes et rideaux. La simplicité quasi monacale de cet appartement témoigne du mépris des Mackintosh pour le matérialisme. Elle révèle aussi leur amour des lignes nettes, des couleurs subtiles et des espaces dégagés. En 1906, ils s'installèrent dans une maison à Florentine Terrace et y créèrent ensemble un environnement extrêmement raffiné, qui s'explique aussi par le fait qu'ils n'avaient pas d'enfant. Les intérieurs éthérés, aujourd'hui reconstitués à la Hunterian Art Gallery,

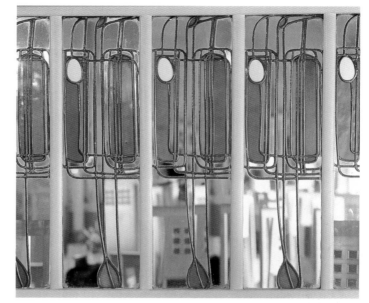

Frieze of leaded mirror-glass panels in the Room de Luxe, Willow Tea Rooms
Fries aus in Blei gefaßten Spiegelglaspaneelen im „Room de Luxe", Willow Tea Rooms
Frise de panneaux en verre-miroir maintenus par des baguettes de plomb dans le «Room de Luxe», Willow Tea Rooms

Waitresses in the Room de Luxe, Willow Tea Rooms, c. 1904
Bedienungen im „Room de Luxe", Willow Tea Rooms
Serveuses dans le «Room de Luxe», Willow Tea Rooms

find an alternative roofing material with the result that the construction was delayed for some six months until the dispute at the quarries had been resolved.

Despite this intransigence and the difficulties it caused him, Blackie's principal request, "that any architectural effect sought should be secured by the massing of the parts rather than by adventitious ornamentation"[30], could not have suited any architect better than Charles Rennie Mackintosh. The interior arrangement of the house was designed prior to the exterior—an early architectural paradigm of "form follows function". Mackintosh juxtaposed traditional architectural elements of the Scottish Baronial style, such as the stairwell tower, against flat unadorned walls (prefiguring the Modern Movement's use of plain reinforced concrete), and created a building that was entirely appropriate, in both its function and aesthetic, to the brief he had been given.

From around 1900, the year of their marriage, to 1906, the Mackintoshes occupied a studio-flat at 120 Mains Street (ill. pp. 72–75). The drawing-room's lightness and spaciousness was the very antithesis of contemporary Edwardian interiors with their heavy furniture and darkening layers of blinds and curtains. The near monastic simplicity of this apartment testified to the Mackintoshes' disregard of materialism and their love of clean lines, delicate colouring and uncluttered space. In 1906, they moved into a house in Florentine Terrace and created together an aesthetic environment which also reflected their childless status. The ethereal and jewel-like interiors, now reconstructed at the Hunterian Art Gallery, give us the sense of a peaceful and chaste spirit at work. How much warmer and homelier the house would have been when occupied by the Mackintoshes, with a fire burning brightly in the grate, their two grey Persian cats sitting either side of the fireplace on specially embroidered cushions, while seed cake was served for afternoon tea. It is certainly difficult to imagine a more suitable setting for Glasgow's foremost aesthetes.

While Mackintosh's reputation continued to grow on the Continent, he was continually frustrated by a lack of personal recognition in the United Kingdom and Glasgow in particular. Although he had been made a partner in Honeyman & Keppie in 1902, became a fellow of the Royal Institute of British Architects (RIBA) in 1906, and in 1908 was elected a fellow of the Royal Incorporation of Architects in Scotland, he could not find sufficient patronage. What few projects he did have, most notably Auchenibert and Cloak, were not fulfilling, given the stylistic limitations that his clients imposed on him. Disillusioned, Mackintosh increasingly drowned his sorrows in drink, much to the distress of his paying clientele. Indeed, Auchenibert

er in der Ausübung seines Berufs doch den Gepflogenheiten einer früheren Zeit verhaftet. Er beschäftigte sich nur ungern mit Zeitplänen, Kalkulationen und knapp bemessenen Budgets. Seine Weigerung oder Unfähigkeit, sich in seiner Arbeit nach den Auflagen seiner Auftraggeber auszurichten, war jedoch weniger durch einen Mangel an Kompetenz begründet als durch Charakterschwächen und die beruflichen Belastungen. Mackintoshs Starrsinn, der wohl als symptomatisch für seine Persönlichkeit angesehen werden muß, kam ihn in seiner späteren beruflichen Tätigkeit teuer zu stehen.

Der Bau von Hill House (Abb. S. 102–111) belegt Mackintoshs beharrliches Streben nach einem vollkommen einheitlichen Entwurf. Bevor er das Projekt in Angriff nahm, bestand er darauf, ein Wochenende im Haus seines Auftraggebers, des Verlegers Walter Blackie, in Dunblane zu verbringen, um zu erfahren, wie die Familie ihr Privatleben organisierte. Bei ihrem ersten Treffen 1902 erwähnte Blackie gegenüber Mackintosh, daß er gern grauen Harling (rauher, mit Kieseln versetzter Zementputz) und ein Schieferdach hätte, beides Elemente schottischer Bautradition. Der Wunsch nach dem Schieferdach wuchs sich allerdings zu einem Problem aus, denn während Hill House gebaut wurde, traten die Arbeiter im Schieferbruch Ballachulish in den Streik. Zur Enttäuschung des ungeduldiger werdenden Blackie bestand Mackintosh auf den Schiefer, und so verzögerte sich die Errichtung des Hauses um sechs Monate.

Trotz der Schwierigkeiten, die Mackintoshs Unnachgiebigkeit ihm bereitete, konnte Blackies Hauptwunsch, „daß man architektonische Wirkungen durch die entsprechende Verteilung der Massen und durch eine vom Zufall abhängige Ausschmückung erreichen solle"[30], keinem Architekten besser entsprechen als Charles Rennie Mackintosh. Das Innere des Hauses wurde zeitlich vor dem Äußeren entworfen—ein frühes architektonisches Musterbeispiel für das Prinzip „die Funktion bestimmt die Form". Mackintosh setzte traditionelle Architekturelemente des schottischen Herrenhausstils, wie den runden Treppenhausturm, neben gerade, schmucklose Mauern (die auf den in der Moderne beliebten Gebrauch von Eisenbeton vorausweisen) und schuf ein Gebäude, das sowohl in seiner Funktion wie in seiner ästhetischen Qualität dem ihm gegebenen Auftrag entsprach.

Von etwa 1900, dem Jahr ihrer Heirat, bis 1906 bewohnte das Ehepaar Mackintosh eine Atelierwohnung in der Mains Street 120 (Abb. S. 72–75). Die Helligkeit und Geräumigkeit des Wohnzimmers bildete geradezu eine Antithese zu den zeitgenössischen Interieurs mit ihren wuchtigen Möbeln und den verdunkelnden, schweren Vorhängen. Die fast mönchische Einfachheit der Wohnung bezeugt Mackintoshs Geringschätzung alles Materiellen und seine Vorliebe für klare Linien, zarte Farben

Hill House, Helensburgh, dining room, 1903
Hill House, Helensburgh, Speisezimmer
Hill House, Helensburgh, salle à manger

Hill House, Helensburgh, bedroom, 1903
Hill House, Helensburgh, Schlafzimmer
Hill House, Helensburgh, chambre à coucher

évoquent un sentiment de paix, de travail et de pureté. Combien plus chaleureuse et accueillante devait être la maison lorsque les Mackintosh l'occupaient: une magnifique flambée crépitait dans l'âtre, deux chats persans gris se faisaient face de part et d'autre de la cheminée, blottis dans les coussins spécialement brodés pour eux, et la maîtresse de maison faisait passer les parts de cake aux noix à l'heure du thé. Sans doute le cadre parfait pour l'avant-garde esthétique de Glasgow.

Mackintosh souffrait de ne pas être reconnu en Grande-Bretagne, et à Glasgow en particulier, alors que sa réputation ne cessait de croître sur le continent. Certes, il était devenu associé de l'agence Honeyman-Keppie-Mackintosh en 1902, membre du Royal Institute of British Architects (RIBA) en 1906 et élu membre du conseil de l'ordre local Royal Incorporation of Architects in Scotland en 1908, mais les commandes n'affluaient pas. Les rares projets qui lui étaient confiés, dont les villas de Auchenibert et Cloak, ne lui procuraient plus de satisfaction en raison des contraintes stylistiques que lui imposaient ses clients. Ayant perdu ses illusions, Mackintosh se mit à noyer son chagrin dans le whisky, au grand mécontentement des clients qui devaient continuer à payer ses honoraires. A Auchenibert les travaux furent achevés sous la responsabilité d'un autre architecte, Mackintosh s'étant désintéressé du projet et réfugié dans l'alcool.

La partie ouest de la Glasgow School of Art (ill. p. 55), achevée en 1909, marque l'apogée de la carrière architecturale de Mackintosh et le début de son déclin. Comme le fait remarquer Mary Newbery Sturrock: «Après l'ouverture de la deuxième partie de la School of Art, Mackintosh n'obtint que de très rares commandes, sans doute parce que Glasgow avait un esprit très province. On ne prenait pas les salons de thé au sérieux, et on trouvait la School of Art très bizarre.»[31] En Europe les Sécessionnistes Hoffmann et Olbrich, qui avaient été fortement influencés par l'Ecossais, avaient des agences florissantes, des disciples et de nombreux mécènes qui leur laissaient toute liberté de création. A Glasgow, «l'art nouveau» de Mackintosh ne faisait guère d'adeptes, et son programme de renaissance de l'architecture écossaise semblait de plus en plus dépassé.

L'irresponsabilité de Mackintosh, son goût immodéré pour la boisson et son caractère désagréable firent perdre des clients à l'agence, qui subissait par ailleurs le contrecoup de la crise économique sévissant à Glasgow: en 1911, son bénéfice annuel n'était plus que de 250 livres, et en 1913, il chuta à 80 livres, un niveau proche de la faillite. En 1913, l'année de la mort de John Honeyman, Mackintosh était dans un tel état physique et mental qu'il était désormais incapable de travailler. Malgré plusieurs mois d'efforts sur le concours de la Jordanhill Demonstration School, son projet était incomplet et irréalisable.

Hill House, Helensburgh, under construction, c. 1903
Hill House, Helensburgh, während der Bauphase
Hill House, Helensburgh, en construction

Hill House, Helensburgh, view from the north
Hill House, Helensburgh, Blick von Norden
Hill House, Helensburgh, vue du nord

was completed by another architect, a resolution due in no small part to Mackintosh's disinterest in the project and increasing reliance on alcohol.

The western section of the Glasgow School of Art (ill. p. 55), completed in 1909, not only marks the high point of Mackintosh's architectural career but also the beginning of his professional decline. Mary Newbery Sturrock noted: "After the second phase of the School of Art opened Mackintosh didn't get much work partly because Glasgow was too provincial. They thought the tea-rooms were a joke and the School of Art very peculiar."[31] On the Continent, his Secessionist contemporaries, Hoffmann and Olbrich, whom he had influenced so greatly, now had flourishing design practices and schools of followers, in addition to a large number of patrons who allowed them the freedom to create modern buildings. In Glasgow, Mackintosh could find few fellow enthusiasts of the "new art" and his vision of a renaissance in Scottish architecture was looking increasingly remote.

Mackintosh's unreliability, his fondness of drink and his uncompromising nature all resulted in several clients of the firm threatening to take their patronage elsewhere. The partnership was also suffering from the general economic downturn experienced in Glasgow at this time—by 1911 its annual profits had fallen sharply to under £250 and by 1913 had dwindled to an almost bankrupting £80. In 1913, the year of John Honeyman's death, Mackintosh was in such a state of mental turmoil and failing health that he was unable to work effectively. After several months of effort, his designs for the Jordanhill Demonstration School competition were either incomplete or unworkable. At the last moment, Keppie was obliged to submit another scheme designed by Graham Henderson, which remarkably won the commission for the demonstration college. It was shortly after this that Mackintosh "resigned" from the firm and the partnership of Honeyman, Keppie & Mackintosh was formally dissolved in June 1914.

Following these events, Mackintosh initially worked from the practice's old premises at 140 Bath Street and later from his home, producing occasional designs for Miss Cranston's tea rooms and entering several competitions, including Liverpool Anglican Cathedral (ill. pp. 98–99) and the College of Domestic Science in Glasgow. When his well-conceived proposal for the "Dough" school (a depreciative Glaswegian term for a college of domestic science) was rejected on a small technical point, he took the criticism of the judges as a personal slight rather than a reflection on his work. It must have been deeply demoralizing to the patriotic Mackintosh to realize that his professional career in Glasgow was all but over and his dream of leading a national architectural revival was out of reach. Glasgow's provincialism had finally won the day.

Daily Record building, detail of the façade
Fassadendetail des Daily-Record-Gebäudes
Détail de la façade de l'immeuble du Daily Record

PAGE 33: Perspective drawing of the façade of the Daily Record building in Glasgow, 1901
SEITE 33: Perspektivischer Fassadenentwurf für das Daily-Record-Gebäude in Glasgow
PAGE 33: Dessin en perspective de l'immeuble du Daily Record à Glasgow

und sparsam möblierte Räume. 1906 bezogen die Mackintoshs ein Haus in der Florentine Terrace und gestalteten gemeinsam eine ästhetische Umgebung, die auch etwas über ihre Kinderlosigkeit aussagt. Die zarten, kostbaren Innenräume, heute in der Hunterian Art Gallery rekonstruiert, vermitteln den Eindruck abgeklärter, asketischer Geistigkeit. Welche Wärme und Behaglichkeit muß das Haus dagegen ausgestrahlt haben, als die Mackintoshs es bewohnten, ein Feuer im Kamin brannte, die zwei grauen Perserkatzen zu beiden Seiten des Kamins auf ihren bestickten Kissen saßen und man zum Tee Kümmelkuchen aß.

Während Mackintoshs Name auf dem Kontinent immer bekannter wurde, blieb in Großbritannien und besonders in Glasgow die Anerkennung aus. Obwohl er 1902 Teilhaber der Firma Honeyman & Keppie geworden war, 1906 Mitglied des Royal Institute of British Architects (RIBA) und 1908 Mitglied der Royal Incorporation of Architects in Schottland wurde, konnte er nicht genug Auftraggeber finden. Die wenigen Projekte, die er zu bearbeiten hatte, vor allem Auchenibert und Cloak, konnten ihn angesichts der stilistischen Einschränkungen, die seine Auftraggeber ihm auferlegten, nicht befriedigen. Auchenibert wurde noch dazu von einem anderen Architekten fertiggestellt, was nicht zuletzt an Mackintoshs mangelndem Interesse an dem Projekt und seiner zunehmenden Alkoholabhängigkeit lag.

Der 1909 vollendete Westflügel der Glasgow School of Art (Abb. S. 55) stellt nicht nur den Höhepunkt seiner Karriere als Architekt dar, er bezeichnet auch den Anfang seines beruflichen Abstiegs. Mary Newbery Sturrock bemerkte: „Nach Beginn der zweiten Bauphase der Glasgow School of Art gab es für Mackintosh nicht mehr viel zu tun, zum Teil weil Glasgow zu provinziell war. Man hielt die Teesalons für einen Witz und die Glasgow School of Art für reichlich seltsam."[31] Im Ausland hatten jetzt die Sezessionisten Hoffmann und Olbrich, auf die er einen starken Einfluß ausgeübt hatte, florierende Architekturbüros, die ihnen ermöglichten, moderne Bauten zu schaffen. In Glasgow fand Mackintosh dagegen nur wenige Gleichgesinnte, die sich für die „neue Kunst" begeisterten, und geriet mit seiner Vision einer Renaissance schottischer Architektur zunehmend ins Abseits.

Mackintoshs Unzuverlässigkeit, seine Trunksucht und Kompromißlosigkeit führten dazu, daß mehrere Kunden der Firma drohten, ihre Aufträge anderweitig zu vergeben. Dazu kam der allgemeine wirtschaftliche Niedergang, den Glasgow um diese Zeit erlebte—1911 war der Jahresgewinn der Firma drastisch auf unter 250 Pfund gesunken und 1913 beinahe auf ein Bankrottniveau von 80 Pfund geschrumpft. 1913, im Todesjahr von John Honeyman, war Mackintosh in einem so schlechten Gesundheitszustand, daß er nicht mehr richtig arbeiten

Au dernier moment Keppie fut obligé de soumettre un autre projet dessiné par Graham Henderson. Ce projet pour un collège scientifique fut déclaré vainqueur. C'est alors que Mackintosh «démissionna» de l'agence, qui fut dissoute officiellement en juin 1914.

Mackintosh conserva les anciens locaux de l'agence au 140 Bath Street pendant quelque temps, avant de se replier chez lui. Il faisait de rares projets pour Miss Cranston et participa à quelques concours, dont la Liverpool Anglican Cathedral (ill. p. 98–99) et le College of Domestic Science de Glasgow. Lorsqu'il perdit ce concours de la «Dough» School, ou «collège pâte à pain» comme l'appelaient les beaux esprits de Glasgow, il crut que l'hostilité du jury était dirigée contre lui et non pas contre ses plans. Nationaliste comme il l'était, Mackintosh ne put qu'être profondément blessé de voir que sa carrière à Glasgow était quasiment parvenue à son terme, et que son rêve d'un renouveau architectural écossais était inexaucé. L'esprit province de Glasgow l'avait finalement emporté.

LES ANNEES D'EXIL

Découragés, les Mackintosh fermèrent leur maison de Glasgow et passèrent l'été de 1914 à Walberswick, où les Newbery s'étaient acheté une petite maison mitoyenne. Il louèrent une pièce dans la maison voisine et un atelier au bord de l'eau, où ils dessinèrent en commun «L'Abri» (ill. p. 121) pour le Willow Tea Rooms. Ils semblent avoir apprécié leur séjour dans ce petit village de la côte du Suffolk. Ils consacraient de longues heures à des études de fleurs et à l'aquarelle. Certaines de ces études devaient être exposées à Liège, Gand et Paris, d'autres devaient faire l'objet d'une publication en Allemagne. Le début de la Première Guerre mondiale empêcha l'exposition parisienne d'avoir lieu. Mackintosh était resté en correspondance avec les Sécessionnistes viennois et avait été invité à les rejoindre en Autriche, mais la déclaration de guerre en août 1914 mit fin à d'éventuels projets d'émigration. La petite communauté artistique de Walberswick déserta le village au début de l'hiver, mais les Mackintosh décidèrent d'y rester pour réfléchir à leur avenir.

La situation stratégique des côtes de l'East Anglia avait conduit le ministère de la Guerre à y imposer des règlements stricts. Les Mackintosh, avec leur tenue «bohème», leur accent «étranger» très prononcé, leur goût pour les longues promenades au crépuscule et leurs rapports épistolaires avec les Sécessionnistes viennois, furent en butte à la suspicion locale, et leurs faits et gestes furent officiellement surveillés par la police. En rentrant d'une promenade tardive, ils trouvèrent même un soldat, baïonnette au fusil, en faction devant leur logement. Lors d'une perquisition, les autorités découvrirent plusieurs lettres postées d'Allemagne et d'Autriche-Hongrie, dont une du Künstlerbund (Ligue des ar-

Disheartened, the Mackintoshes closed up their house in Glasgow and spent the summer of 1914 in Walberswick, where the Newberys had bought a semi-detached villa. They rented a room in the adjacent house and a riverside studio in which they designed "The Dug-Out" room (ill. p. 121) for the Willow Tea Rooms. By all accounts, they seem to have initially enjoyed their break in this small coastal Suffolk village, devoting the majority of their time to flower studies and watercolouring. Some of the Walberswick studies were painted for exhibitions in Liège, Ghent and Paris, while others were executed for a proposed German publication. Due to the outbreak of World War I, however, these studies were not shown in the French capital. Mackintosh continued actively corresponding with the Secessionists and had been invited to join their movement in Vienna, but the war's beginning in mid-August ended any ideas the Mackintoshes might have harboured about emigration. When the seasonal artistic community left Walberswick for the winter, the Mackintoshes remained to rethink and replan their future.

Due to the strategic importance of East Anglia's coastline, strict regulations regarding wartime security were imposed. The Mackintoshes, with their "artistic" clothes, strong "foreign" accents, penchant for long evening walks and their known connection with the Viennese Secessionists, aroused local suspicion and their movements were put under official police observation. On their return from a walk at dusk one evening, the Mackintoshes found a soldier stationed with a bayonet outside their lodgings. The authorities examined their papers and found several letters from Germany and Austria including one from the *Künstlerbund*. This resulted in Mackintosh being taken into police custody where he was later brought before a tribunal and accused of spying.

Thanks to the intervention of friends, Mackintosh was eventually released and it was only after persistent lobbying, a statement to the Home Secretary, and pressure from Lord Curzon (later Foreign Minister), that the Mackintoshes were able to clear their names. Given this, the authorities still decreed that the Mackintoshes were not allowed to live in Suffolk, Norfolk or Cambridgeshire nor, like other artists, near any coastline, major road or railway track. They were ordered to state where they intended to go and to report themselves to the police once they had got there. This terrible ordeal, described by Mackintosh as "the absurd outrage on the rights of perfectly loyal subjects"[32] was clearly an affront to his patriotism and left the couple with no alternative but to seek refuge in London.

The Mackintoshes left Suffolk and arrived in London in 1915 and this became their home for the next eight years. For the first few weeks of this period,

konnte. Trotz monatelanger angestrengter Bemühung blieben seine Entwürfe für die Jordanhill-Demonstration-School-Ausschreibung unvollständig oder undurchführbar. Keppie mußte im letzten Augenblick einen anderen, von Graham Henderson erarbeiteten Entwurf einreichen, der dann tatsächlich angenommen wurde. Kurz darauf zog sich Mackintosh aus der Firma zurück; die Partnerschaft Honeyman, Keppie & Mackintosh wurde im Juni 1914 aufgelöst.

Danach arbeitete Mackintosh zunächst weiter in den ehemaligen Räumlichkeiten der Firma in der Bath Street 140 und dann zu Hause. Gelegentlich fertigte er Entwürfe für Miss Cranstons Teesalons und beteiligte sich an Wettbewerben, unter anderem für die Anglican Cathedral in Liverpool (Abb. S. 98–99) und das College for Domestic Science in Glasgow. Als sein wohldurchdachter Plan für die „Dough"-Schule (dough = Teig, ein pejorativer Glasgower Ausdruck für eine Hauswirtschaftsschule) wegen eines geringfügigen technischen Problems abgelehnt wurde, glaubte er, die abweisende Einstellung der Jury gälte nicht dem Entwurf, sondern ihm persönlich. Der patriotische Mackintosh muß zutiefst entmutigt gewesen sein, als er erkannte, daß seine Laufbahn in Glasgow so gut wie beendet war und daß sein Traum, einer nationalen Wiedergeburt der Architektur den Weg zu weisen, keine Aussicht auf Verwirklichung mehr hatte.

IM EXIL

Entmutigt verließen die Mackintoshs ihr Haus in Glasgow und verbrachten den Sommer 1914 in Walberswick in Suffolk, wo die Newberys eine Doppelhaushälfte erworben hatten. Neben einem Zimmer im Nachbarhaus mieteten sie auch ein Atelier am Flußufer an, in dem der Entwurf des „Dug-Out"-Raums (Abb. S. 121) für die Willow Tea Rooms entstand. Den größten Teil ihrer Zeit widmeten sie dem Zeichnen von Blumen und der Aquarellmalerei. Einige der in Walberswick entstandenen Zeichnungen waren für Ausstellungen in Lüttich, Gent und Paris gedacht, andere für eine geplante deutsche Publikation. Der Ausbruch des Ersten Weltkriegs verhinderte jedoch die Ausstellung der Arbeiten in der französischen Hauptstadt. Mackintosh, der weiterhin in reger Korrespondenz mit der Wiener Sezession stand, hatte das Angebot erhalten, sich ihrer Künstlergruppe anzuschließen. Der Kriegsbeginn Mitte August 1914 setzte jedoch allen Gedanken an eine Emigration, die das Ehepaar Mackintosh vielleicht erwogen haben mochte, ein Ende. Als die Künstlerkolonie zum Winter ihre Zelte in Walberswick abbrach, blieben die Mackintoshs zurück, um für die Zukunft neue Pläne zu schmieden.

Aufgrund der strategischen Bedeutung der ostenglischen Küste waren strenge Sicherheitsvorschriften erlassen worden. Die Mackintoshs erregten

tistes). Mackintosh fut mis en détention préventive, traîné devant un tribunal et accusé d'espionnage.

Il fut finalement relâché grâce à l'intervention de ses amis. Mais il fallut toute une série de démarches, une déclaration au ministère de l'Intérieur et l'intervention de Lord Curzon (qui devait devenir ministre des Affaires Etrangères) pour que les Mackintosh soient lavés de tout soupçon. Ce qui ne les empêcha pas d'être interdits de séjour dans le Suffolk, le Norfolk et le Cambridgeshire, ainsi que sur les côtes et aux abords des grandes routes et des voies de chemin de fer, comme tous les peintres d'ailleurs. Ils devaient informer les autorités de leurs déplacements et signaler leur présence à la police dès leur arrivée. Cette expérience pénible fut considérée par Mackintosh comme «une atteinte odieuse aux droits légitimes des loyaux sujets de Sa Majesté»[32]. Cet affront fait à son patriotisme ne lui laissait d'autre choix que de chercher refuge à Londres.

Les Mackintosh arrivèrent donc dans la capitale anglaise en 1915 et y vécurent huit ans. Au début, Mackintosh travailla au King's College pour Patrick Geddes et dessina des plans de villes: le professeur Geddes réfléchissait à l'époque sur des plans d'urbanisme en Inde. Philip Mairet, qui partageait un atelier avec Mackintosh à l'époque, se souvient de lui en ces termes: «Il ne m'était pas vraiment sympathique, sans doute parce qu'il était perpétuellement imbibé d'alcool... Il me fit l'impression d'un homme brillant tombé dans la déchéance.»[33] C'est peut-être par l'entremise de Patrick Geddes que Mackintosh fut invité à passer six mois à Bombay ou Calcutta, pour y travailler à des projets urbains. Il déclina l'offre pour rester à Londres.

L'œuvre de l'Ecossais était pratiquement inconnue dans la capitale, et il lui fut très difficile d'obtenir des commandes à cause de la morosité économique engendrée par le conflit mondial. Les Mackintosh se firent pourtant des amis dans la colonie artistique de Chelsea. Ils habitaient alors à Oakley Street et louaient deux ateliers à Glebe Place. Ils prenaient leur repas du soir au *Blue Cockatoo*, le restaurant bohème de Cheyne Walk. Ils y rencontrèrent George Bernard Shaw (1856–1950), Augustus John (1878–1961), J. D. Fergusson (1874–1961) et sa femme Margaret Morris.

Pour compléter la petite rente que sa mère avait laissée à Margaret, Mackintosh se mit à l'aquarelle et à la création de tissus. Il conçut des motifs pour W. Foxton's Limited et Sefton's Limited, firmes textiles parmi les plus novatrices de l'époque. Pour cette production Mackintosh eut principalement recours à des plantes stylisées et à des formes géométriques simples. Le travail était relativement bien payé: 200 livres sterling pour la seule année 1920. Mais ses succès dans cette discipline relativement mineure ne suffisaient pas à satisfaire ses ambitions. Pour lui, l'architecture était l'art suprême, puisqu'il pensait comme William Richard Lethaby que

Polyanthus, Walberswick, watercolour, 1915
Gartenrosen, Walberswick, Aquarell
Roses de jardin, Walberswick, aquarelle
25.8 x 20.2 cm

SHOP AND OFFICE BLOCK IN AN ARCADED STREET · CHARLES RENNIE MACKINTOSH FRIBA · ARCHITECT

Mackintosh worked for Patrick Geddes at King's College on streetscape plans relating to the professor's own Indian town planning schemes. Philip Mairet, who shared a studio with Mackintosh at the time, recalls: "His personality, unfortunately, did not make a very congenial impression on me—but this was chiefly because his aura was suffused with the alcoholic potations to which he was addicted (...) The impression that remained with me was that of a brilliant man who was a tragic case."[33] Later in 1915, Mackintosh was invited to spend six months in either Bombay or Calcutta by the Indian government to work on reconstruction schemes. He declined this opportunity and remained in London.

In the capital, Mackintosh's work was practically unknown and with the general wartime economic gloom he found it exceedingly difficult to attract any business. The Mackintoshes did, however, find friendship in Chelsea's artistic colony. They took lodgings in Oakley Street and worked in two rented studios in Glebe Place, dining every evening at the Blue Cockatoo, an infamous Chelsea meeting place in Cheyne Walk. Among their circle of friends at this time were George Bernard Shaw (1856–1950), Augustus John (1878–1961), J. D. Fergusson (1874–1961) and his wife Margaret Morris.

Attempting to supplement Margaret's small private income left to her by her mother, Mackintosh turned his attentions to watercolour painting and textile design, creating fabric patterns for both W. Foxton's Limited and Sefton's Limited, among the most innovative British textile manufacturers of the period. In the designs he produced for these two companies, Mackintosh mainly used stylized plant forms as well as bold geometric patterns. This work was relatively lucrative and in 1920 alone he was paid £200 for his textile designs. However, his success in this somewhat lesser discipline did not console him or alleviate his frustration. To Mackintosh, architecture was the highest art, believing, as Lethaby did, that "architecture is the synthesis of the fine arts, the commune of all the crafts".

Mackintosh's hope was somewhat restored when

wegen ihrer „Künstlergarderobe", ihres „ausländischen"—nämlich schottischen—Akzents, den langen abendlichen Spaziergängen und ihrer nicht unbekannt gebliebenen Verbindung zur Wiener Sezession Argwohn im Ort, so daß sie polizeilich überwacht wurden. Bei der Rückkehr von einem ihrer abendlichen Spaziergänge fanden sie vor ihrem Haus einen Soldaten mit aufgepflanztem Bajonett vor. Die Polizei durchsuchte ihre Unterlagen und fand mehrere Briefe aus Deutschland und Österreich, darunter einen vom Künstlerbund. Mackintosh wurde daraufhin verhaftet und wegen Spionage angeklagt.

Dank der Fürsprache von Freunden wurde Mackintosh aus der Untersuchungshaft entlassen. Aber erst nach einer an das Innenministerium gerichteten Eingabe und Druck seitens Lord Curzons (dem späteren Außenminister) konnte sich das Ehepaar Mackintosh von allem Verdacht befreien. Die Behörden verfügten dennoch, daß die Mackintoshs weder in Suffolk, Norfolk oder Cambridgeshire noch, wie andere Künstler, in unmittelbarer Küstennähe, an einer Hauptverkehrsstraße oder einem Eisenbahngleis wohnen durften. Sie mußten angeben, wo sie sich aufzuhalten gedachten und sich dort umgehend bei der Polizei melden. Diese quälende Situation, die Mackintosh als „eine absurde Verletzung der Rechte absolut loyaler Staatsbürger"[32] bezeichnete, stellte eine Beleidigung seines Patriotismus dar und ließ dem Ehepaar keine andere Möglichkeit, als in London Zuflucht zu suchen.

Die Mackintoshs ließen sich 1915 in London nieder, wo sie für die folgenden acht Jahre ihren Wohnsitz haben sollten. Während der ersten Wochen arbeitete Mackintosh zunächst für Patrick Geddes, Professor am King's College, an Plänen, die mit Geddes' Stadtplanungsprojekten in Indien zusammenhingen. Philip Mairet, der sich damals ein Atelier mit Mackintosh teilte, erinnert sich: „Seine Persönlichkeit machte leider keinen sehr sympathischen Eindruck auf mich—das lag aber vor allem daran, daß sein Erscheinen von seiner Trunksucht bestimmt wurde (...) Ich behielt von ihm den Ein-

tement et refusait de l'avouer. Jessie Newbery (1864–1948) trouva un médecin compréhensif, lui expliqua que Mackintosh était un architecte de renom qui traversait une passe difficile et réussit ainsi à faire hospitaliser son ami. Le traitement au radium donna de bons résultats et Mackintosh put quitter l'hôpital. Margaret avait trouvé un logement à Willow Road, Hampstead. Margaret Morris fit faire au malade des exercices pour lui réapprendre à parler, mais son état ne fit qu'empirer et il perdit définitivement l'usage de la parole. Une querelle avec la propriétaire, sans doute pour une affaire d'arriéré de loyer, obligea les Mackintosh à déménager à nouveau.

Un ami de longue date, Desmond Chapman-Huston, leur proposa un toit temporaire—les deux derniers étages de sa maison du 72 Porchester Square—pendant qu'il était à l'étranger. La santé de Mackintosh ne cessait de se dégrader, et il entra à la clinique du 26 Porchester Square. C'est là qu'il mourut le 10 décembre 1928 à l'âge de 60 ans. Il fut incinéré le lendemain au cimetière Golders Green, en présence de 6 personnes seulement. On sait que Margaret voulait disperser ses cendres dans la mer à Port-Vendres, et elle le fit sans doute lors d'un séjour ultérieur en France. Elle retourna ensuite vivre à Chelsea, où elle mena une vie tranquille jusqu'à sa mort, le 10 janvier 1933. Après son décès, on fit l'inventaire des ateliers de Glebe Place, qui contenaient de nombreux dessins d'architecture, des meubles, des esquisses, 26 aquarelles et 5 tableaux de fleurs. Le commissaire-priseur considéra que tout était absolument sans valeur et sans intérêt, et l'ensemble fut estimé à 88 livres, 16 shillings et 2 pence.

Une exposition commémorative Mackintosh fut organisée en mai 1933 à Glasgow, aux galeries McLellan qui avaient remplacé les Corporation Galleries. Elle dura trois semaines, et rendit à Mackintosh une part de l'hommage que ses concitoyens auraient pu lui manifester plus tôt. Il n'empêche qu'on le considérait encore, à tort, comme un décorateur Art nouveau. Mais en fait Mackintosh fut un marginal qui ne se reconnaissait dans aucun mouvement. Et il pensait que l'inspiration personnelle conduirait plus sûrement à la beauté que la recherche de l'universel, croyance centrale de la modernité.

La méthode de travail de Mackintosh, qui acceptait et réconciliait les potentialités scientifiques et les besoins spirituels, devait beaucoup à la philosophie métaphysique hégélienne du XIXème siècle. Cette croyance se manifestait dans la recherche de l'unité organique totale dans le projet créatif. C'est par l'attention portée aux visées sociales et fonctionnelles d'une part, et par l'aspect spirituel de son œuvre de l'autre, que se manifeste l'indéniable génie de Mackintosh.

La meilleure preuve de son originalité est l'absence de postérité esthétique. Tout au long de sa vie, il

Mont-Louis, flower study, watercolour, 1925
Mont-Louis, Blumenstudie, Aquarell
Mont-Louis, Etude de fleurs, aquarelle
25.8 x 20.2 cm

Clock designed for Hill House,
Helensburgh, 1905

Uhr, entworfen für das Hill House
in Helensburgh

Pendule conçue pour Hill House
à Helensburgh

of the two upper floors in his house at 72 Porchester Square while he was abroad. Mackintosh's health continued to worsen and he was admitted into a nursing home at 26 Porchester Square, where he died on 10 December 1928 at the age of sixty. His cremation the following day at Golders Green Cemetery was attended by only six people. It is known that Margaret wished to scatter his ashes on the sea at Port-Vendres and it is highly probable that she did this when she later visited the harbour town. Margaret returned to live in Chelsea where she led a quiet life until her death on 10 January 1933. After her death, the contents of the Mackintoshes' Glebe Place studios, which included numerous architectural drawings, furniture, sketches, twenty-six watercolours and five flower paintings, were deemed virtually worthless by the assessor and valued at £88 16s 2d.

Later in May 1933, a memorial exhibition of Mackintosh's work was staged at the McLellan Galleries (formerly the Corporation Galleries) in Glasgow. The three-week show granted Mackintosh some of the long-awaited acclaim he so richly deserved from the inhabitants of his native city. Even so, many people still regarded him, incorrectly, as an Art Nouveau designer. Indeed, Mackintosh worked outside of all mainstream stylistic movements, believing that individualism would impart quality in design more readily than universality, a maxim which was also one of the central tenets of the Modern Movement.

The methodology evolved by Mackintosh, which accepted and reconciled the potential of science with the needs of the soul, mirrored the 19th century metaphysical philosophy of Hegelianism. This belief system was manifest in his objective of achieving a total organic unity of design. Through his careful consideration of the functional and social purposes as well as the spiritual effect of his work, Mackintosh's unquestionable genius is revealed.

The individualistic quality of his work meant, however, that he never had a school of followers who could have perpetuated his vision. Throughout his life, Mackintosh remained committed to his humanist goals, and was in complete accordance with Lethaby, who believed "a reasonable building is not necessarily a series of boxes or a structure of steel. The most scientific and sensible building for given conditions might still be of brick and thatch".[37] Mackintosh's opposition to the Modern Movement's drift towards the technologically obsessed and ultimately alienating International Style isolated him from the design debate in the latter years of his career. Despite this, however, he continued to maintain that appropriateness, or as he termed it "seemliness", should be at the heart of all design considerations.

Mackintosh's patriotism and obstinacy compelled him to remain in Scotland, even though it is likely näheren Umgebung malte. Die meisten dieser Bilder, wie *Le Fort Maillert* (Abb. S. 167) und *La Ville*, Port-Vendres (Abb. S. 161), offenbaren durch die flächige Farbgebung und die Themenwahl die Hand des Architekten.

Im Mai 1927 mußte Margaret aus medizinischen Gründen nach London zurückkehren. Mackintosh, der sie sehr vermißte, blieb allein in Port-Vendres und arbeitete an seinen Aquarellen. In den zwei Monaten der Trennung schrieb er zahlreiche Briefe, die ihre zärtliche Beziehung, ihre hoffnungslose finanzielle Situation und seine tiefe Depression erkennen lassen. Sie waren praktisch mittellos: Mackintosh mußte sich um Portokosten und Geld für Malutensilien Sorgen machen. Zuletzt klagte er darüber, daß seine Zunge geschwollen und mit Bläschen übersät sei, was seiner Ansicht nach am französischen Tabak lag. Nachdem Margaret im Juli aus London zurückgekehrt war, blieben sie in Mont-Louis, bis Mackintosh krank wurde.

Im Herbst 1927 kehrten sie nach London zurück, wo man bei Charles Zungenkrebs diagnostizierte. Da er die Behandlung nicht bezahlen konnte und zu stolz war, dies mitzuteilen, verzögerte sich seine Aufnahme in ein städtisches Krankenhaus. Erst als Jessie Newbery (1864–1948) dem verständnisvollen Arzt erklärte, daß Mackintosh ein großer Architekt sei, der sich in finanziellen Schwierigkeiten befände, konnte er sich im Krankenhaus einer Radiumtherapie unterziehen. Nach seiner Entlassung—anscheinend hatte sich sein Zustand deutlich gebessert—fand Margaret eine Unterkunft in der Willow Road in Hampstead. Hier machte Margaret Morris Sprechübungen mit ihm, aber leider verschlechterte sich sein Zustand derart, daß er schließlich überhaupt nicht mehr sprechen konnte. Nach einer Meinungsverschiedenheit mit der Hauswirtin, vermutlich wegen rückständiger Mietzahlungen, mußten sie ausziehen.

Ihr langjähriger Freund Desmond Chapman-Huston bot ihnen für die Dauer seines Auslandsaufenthalts die beiden oberen Etagen seines Hauses am Porchester Square 72 an. Mackintoshs Befinden verschlechterte sich jedoch zusehends, so daß er sich in ein Pflegeheim am Porchester Square 26 begeben mußte, wo er am 10. Dezember 1928 im Alter von sechzig Jahren starb. Der Einäscherung auf dem Friedhof Golders Green am Tag danach wohnten nur sechs Personen bei. Es heißt, daß Margaret seine Asche bei Port-Vendres ins Meer streuen wollte, was sie sehr wahrscheinlich auch getan hat, als sie später dorthin fuhr. Sie zog wieder nach Chelsea, wo sie bis zu ihrem Tod am 10. Januar 1933 ein zurückgezogenes Leben führte. Nach ihrem Tod wurde ihre Hinterlassenschaft, zahlreiche Architekturzeichnungen, Einrichtungsgegenstände, Skizzen, sechsundzwanzig Aquarelle und fünf Blumenbilder von einem Gutachter als praktisch wertlos erachtet und auf 88 Pfund, 16 Shilling und 2 Pence geschätzt.

est resté fidèle à ses idéaux humanistes. Il ne pouvait que partager le point de vue de Lethaby: «Un bâtiment rationnel n'est pas nécessairement un assemblage de boîtes ou une structure d'acier. Dans certaines conditions, l'architecture scientifique et rationnelle peut se contenter de la brique et du chaume.»[37]

Mackintosh désapprouvait la dérive technologique du Mouvement Moderne, qui devait conduire au splendide isolement du Style International. Cette attitude l'écarta du débat architectural vers la fin de sa vie. Il n'en continua pas moins à soutenir que la satisfaction des besoins, qu'il appelait «convenance», était au cœur du processus créatif.

Par nationalisme et obstination, Mackintosh voulut rester en Ecosse. Il ne fait pas de doute que s'il avait émigré en Europe ou aux Etats-Unis, il aurait obtenu la reconnaissance qu'il recherchait désespérément. Il faut bien voir aussi que sa personnalité originale, qui lui a valu des succès précoces, fut aussi la cause de son échec en lui enlevant toute influence réelle sur le Mouvement Moderne naissant, et en le condamnant à gâcher son talent. Père fondateur de la Modernité organique, Charles Rennie Mackintosh laisse un héritage d'une pertinence toujours actuelle: une vision holistique et humaniste du projet architectural, qui appréhende le monde comme un organisme vivant complexe et en respecte les dimensions sociales, écologiques et spirituelles.

Charles Rennie Mackintosh, c. 1910

he would have received the recognition he so desperately desired had he emigrated to the Continent or, indeed, the United States of America. Furthermore, his own idiosyncratic character not only enabled him to rise early on in his career, but was the central cause of his downfall, severely hindering his potential influence within the Modern Movement and guaranteeing the inevitable and tragic waste of his talent. As one of the founding fathers of organic Modernism, however, Charles Rennie Mackintosh left an important legacy that is extremely relevant to our own times—a holistic and humanist approach to design that comprehends the world as a complex living organism and respects the personal, social, environmental and spiritual realities found within it.

Im Mai 1933 fand in der McLellan Galerie (den früheren Corporation Galleries) in Glasgow eine Mackintosh-Gedächtnisausstellung statt. Die dreiwöchige Schau verschaffte Mackintosh postum die so lang ersehnte und mehr als verdiente Anerkennung in seiner Heimatstadt. Für viele galt er zu Unrecht als reiner Jugendstil-Künstler. In Wirklichkeit war Mackintosh unabhängig von allen modischen Stilrichtungen, da er die Auffassung vertrat, daß Qualität im Entwurf eher aus individuellen als aus universellen Bestrebungen resultiert—ein Leitgedanke der Moderne.

Die von Mackintosh entwickelte Formensprache, welche die Erkenntnisse der Wissenschaft aufnahm und mit den Bedürfnissen der Seele versöhnte, spiegelte die metaphysische Philosophie des Hegelianismus wider. Dieses Denken zeigte sich in seinem Bestreben, bei seinen Arbeiten eine allumfassende organische Einheit zu erreichen. In der sorgsamen Abwägung der funktionalen und sozialen Zielsetzung sowie der geistigen Wirkung seiner Arbeit erweist sich Mackintoshs unbezweifelbare Genialität.

Die individualistische Komponente seiner Arbeit bedingte, daß er nie eine Anhängerschaft fand, die seine Vision hätte bewahren können. Zeitlebens blieb er seinen humanistischen Zielen verpflichtet und stimmte mit Lethaby überein, der meinte, „daß ein vernünftiges Gebäude nicht notwendigerweise aus einer Reihe von Kästen oder einer Stahlkonstruktion bestehen muß. Unter bestimmten Bedingungen könnte das wissenschaftlichste und vernünftigste Gebäude immer noch aus Backstein und Stroh bestehen."[37] Mit seinem Widerstand gegen die Entwicklung der Moderne in Richtung auf den technisch bestimmten Internationalen Stil schloß sich Mackintosh von der aktuellen Architekturdebatte aus. Er blieb bei seiner Auffassung, daß Angemessenheit oder, wie er es nannte, „Schicklichkeit" im Mittelpunkt aller Überlegungen zum Thema Design stehen sollte.

Sein Patriotismus und sein Starrsinn zwangen ihn, in Schottland zu bleiben, auch wenn er wahrscheinlich die ersehnte Anerkennung auf dem Kontinent oder in den USA gefunden hätte. Seine Eigenwilligkeit war nicht nur die Ursache seines frühen beruflichen Erfolges, sondern auch der Grund für sein Scheitern: Sie hinderte ihn daran, innerhalb der Moderne Einfluß auszüüben und führte zu der tragischen Vergeudung seines Talents. Als einer der Väter der „organischen" Moderne freilich hinterließ Charles Rennie Mackintosh ein Vermächtnis, das für unsere Zeit größte Bedeutung hat—eine ganzheitliche, humane Auffassung des Designs, die die Welt als einen komplexen lebendigen Organismus begreift und die persönlichen, sozialen, ökologischen und geistigen Gegebenheiten respektiert.

Glasgow Herald Building 1893–1895

The water tower
Der Wasserturm
Le château d'eau

This corner site extension, which was commissioned by the Glasgow Herald and designed between 1893–1894, provided not only newspaper offices but also shops and warehousing. Although only a junior draughtsman at Honeyman & Keppie at the time, the extent of Mackintosh's involvement in the design of this scheme is betrayed by its water tower, the asymmetrical fenestration and characteristic carved organic decoration. Even so, he would have worked within the framework of the firm's principles. Sympathetic to the surrounding architecture, the building's soaring "campanile" tower, topped by a curious flattened cupola, hid from view an 8,000 gallon water tank which was intended as a fire safety precaution. Other features included fire-resistant concrete flooring and a hydropneumatic lift. *The British Architect* journal commented in 1896 that the building "ranks first of any modern building we know of for boldness and originality of treatment allied with some sense of architectural dignity. It verges dangerously on the confines of pure eccentricity in parts, but this does not sensibly injure its architectural quality."

Der Eckanbau des Glasgow Herald, zwischen 1893 und 1894 von dem Architekturbüro Honeyman & Keppie entworfen, beherbergte neben den Redaktionsbüros der Zeitung auch Ladenlokale und Lagerräume. Obwohl Mackintosh damals nur als untergeordneter Entwurfszeichner bei Honeyman & Keppie tätig war, belegen die Formgebung des Wasserturms, die asymmetrische Fensteranordnung und die für ihn charakteristischen organischen Steinmetzdekore das Ausmaß seiner Beteiligung an diesem Projekt. Der harmonisch in die benachbarte Architektur eingefügte Wasserturm mit seiner ungewöhnlich abgeflachten Kuppel verbarg als Brandschutzvorkehrung einen 36 000 Liter fassenden Wassertank. Weitere architektonische Besonderheiten waren der feuersichere Zementfußboden und ein hydropneumatischer Aufzug. 1896 schrieb die Fachzeitschrift *The British Architect*, daß das Gebäude „wegen seiner Kühnheit und Originalität in Verein mit einem Gefühl für architektonische Würde unter allen modernen Gebäuden, die wir kennen, einzigartig ist. Es nähert sich in manchen Teilen gefährlich den Bereichen reiner Exzentrizität, aber das beeinträchtigt kaum seine architektonische Qualität."

Commandée par le Glasgow Herald et conçue en 1893–1894, cette extension à un angle de rue abritait non seulement les bureaux du journal, mais aussi des boutiques et des entrepôts. Mackintosh, alors simple projeteur à l'agence Honeyman & Keppie, semble avoir joué un rôle considérable dans le projet. On devine son intervention dans la tour d'angle qui contient le château d'eau, dans le rythme asymétrique des baies et dans la sculpture décorative «organique». Il ne s'est guère éloigné pour autant du style habituel de l'agence. Le grand donjon «campanile» coiffé d'une étrange coupole aplatie s'intègre bien à l'architecture environnante. Il contenait une citerne de 36 000 litres, comme l'exigeaient les règlements de sécurité-incendie. Le bâtiment comportait aussi des dalles en béton anti-incendie et un ascenseur hydropneumatique. En 1896, la revue *The British Architect* fit le commentaire suivant: «Son audace, son originalité et la noblesse de son style le classent devant tous les bâtiments modernes que nous connaissons. Il frôle parfois dangereusement l'excentricité, mais cela n'enlève rien à sa qualité architecturale.»

Perspective drawing, 1893–94
Perspektivische Entwurfszeichnung
Dessin en perspective

Martyrs' Public School 1895–1896

Detail of the cornice
Detail des Dachgesims
La corniche, détail

Commissioned by the School Board in 1895, the Martyrs' Public School provided accommodation for around 1,000 children. The project was highly constrained by the relatively small site and meagre budget of only £10,000. Despite this, Mackintosh was able to imbue the school with an identifiable character through his own individual style. Particularly distinctive are the roof trusses and striking roof supporting brackets which are oriental in flavour and jut out from the wall by nearly a metre. The building's mass was visually lightened by the three white octagonal and ogee crowned elements on the roof, which hid the ventilation system. Although the design of this building is rather restrained, relying on earlier Scottish precedents, the inclusion of these innovative elements presages Mackintosh's later architecture. This project must, therefore, be considered a transitional work.

Die von der örtlichen Schulbehörde 1895 in Auftrag gegebene Martyrs' Public School sollte Platz für etwa 1000 Schüler bieten. Das relativ kleine Grundstück und das knappe Budget von nur 10000 Pfund setzten dem Bauprojekt jedoch von vornherein enge Grenzen. Trotzdem gelang es Mackintosh, der Schule einen unverwechselbaren Charakter zu geben. Besonders bemerkenswert ist die Dachkonstruktion mit dem orientalisch anmutenden Gesims, das fast einen Meter hervorragt. Die Blockhaftigkeit des Gebäudes wird durch die drei weißen achteckigen, pagodenförmigen Dachaufsätze, hinter denen sich das Belüftungssystem verbarg, optisch aufgelockert. Obwohl der Gesamtentwurf noch stark an frühere schottische Vorbilder angelehnt ist, weist die Aufnahme dieser innovativen Elemente bereits auf spätere Arbeiten Mackintoshs hin. Insgesamt muß der Entwurf als Übergangswerk betrachtet werden.

La Martyrs' Public School commanditée par le Comité Scolaire de la ville en 1895 devait accueillir 1000 enfants environ. Les contraintes étaient très strictes: la parcelle était petite et le budget ne dépassait pas les 10000 livres sterling. Mackintosh n'en a pas moins réussi à donner à cette école une originalité certaine empreinte de son style propre. On remarque particulièrement les fermes de la charpente et les étonnants corbeaux de l'auvent, en saillie d'un mètre environ, et qui donnent à l'ensemble une touche orientale. La masse du bâtiment était allégée par trois éléments blancs sur le toit, de forme octogonale et à couverture ogivale, qui contenaient le système de ventilation. Bien que le style de l'école soit plutôt sobre, et dans la lignée du style traditionnel écossais, l'utilisation de certains éléments novateurs annonce l'architecture ultérieure de Mackintosh. On peut donc la considérer comme une œuvre de transition.

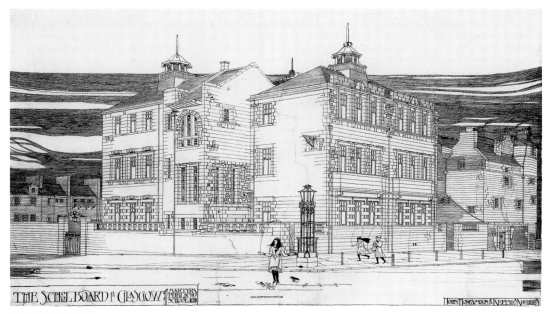

Perspective drawing, 1895

Perspektivische Entwurfszeichnung

Dessin en perspective

General view from Parson Street

Gesamtansicht von der Parson Street

Vue générale depuis Parson Street

The 91–93 Buchanan Street premises were acquired by Catherine Cranston in 1895. A year later, she contracted the Edinburgh builder, George Washington Brown, to rebuild the property and it was opened as tea rooms the following summer in 1897. Having already commissioned George Walton & Co. to decorate and furnish the new site, Cranston met Mackintosh in 1896 and asked him to produce three large-scale stencilled wall decorations for the ladies' tea room, the luncheon room and the smoking gallery. These rooms are believed to have been on different floors and all three works, which symbolized the transition from earth to heaven, would have been visible from the stairwell. The wall decorations—avant-garde for their day—were the cause of much controversy and helped to ensure that the tea rooms became an overnight success. It is likely that Mackintosh also contributed several lighting designs to this project.

1895 erwarb Catherine Cranston die Räumlichkeiten in der Buchanan Street 91–93. Im darauffolgenden Jahr beauftragte sie den Edinburgher Bauunternehmer George Washington Brown mit deren Umbau, und schon im Sommer 1897 eröffnete sie hier ihren ersten Teesalon. Erst nachdem sie George Walton & Co. verpflichtet hatte, die neuen Räume einzurichten und zu möblieren, lernte sie 1896 Mackintosh kennen und bat ihn, drei große Schablonen-Wanddekors für das Damen-Teezimmer, den Speissaal und die Rauchergalerie zu entwerfen. Alle drei Werke, die die Verbindung zwischen Himmel und Erde symbolisierten, waren vom Treppenhaus aus zu sehen, befanden sich aber vermutlich auf verschiedenen Ebenen. Die für ihre Zeit avantgardistisch anmutenden Wanddekors führten zu heftigen Kontroversen und trugen nicht unwesentlich dazu bei, den schlagartig einsetzenden geschäftlichen Erfolg des Teesalons zu sichern. Vermutlich hat Mackintosh auch mehrere Leuchten für dieses Projekt entworfen.

Catherine Cranston acheta le 91–93 Buchanan Street en 1895. Un an plus tard, elle demandait à George Washington Brown, entrepreneur à Edimbourg, de reconstruire les locaux. On y inaugura un salon de thé l'été suivant, en 1897. Bien qu'elle eut déjà retenu George Walton & Co. pour la décoration et l'ameublement, Mademoiselle Cranston demanda à Mackintosh en 1896 de concevoir trois grandes décorations au pochoir: pour le salon de thé des dames, pour la salle à manger, et pour le fumoir. On pense que ces pièces se trouvaient à différents niveaux, et que les trois œuvres au pochoir, symbolisant le passage de la terre au ciel, se voyaient de la cage d'escalier. Ces décorations murales, très avant-gardistes pour leur temps, suscitèrent de nombreuses controverses et assurèrent au salon de thé un succès immédiat. Il est vraisemblable que Mackintosh est également intervenu dans la conception de l'éclairage.

STENCILLED WALL DECORATIONS FOR BUCHANAN STREET TEA ROOMS, 1896

STENCILLED WALL
DECORATIONS FOR
BUCHANAN STREET TEA ROOMS
1896

TOP: Design for the stencilled wall decoration
in the ladies' tea room, 1896

OBEN: Entwurfszeichnung für das Schablonen-
Wanddekor im Damen-Teezimmer

CI-DESSUS: Projet de décoration au pochoir
pour le salon de thé des dames

RIGHT: The ladies' tea room, c. 1897

RECHTS: Das Damen-Teezimmer

A DROITE: Le salon de thé des dames

Detail of the wrought-iron grille at the main entrance
Detail des schmiedeeisernen Zaunes am Haupteingang
La grille en fer forgé de l'entrée principale, détail

Glasgow School of Art
1897–1899 & 1907–1909

By the early 1900s, the Glasgow School of Art's accommodation at the Corporation Galleries was insufficient to cope with the increasing number of students. Francis H. Newbery, the School's director, called a meeting of the Governors in September 1895 to discuss the raising of funds for a new building. By February 1896, the sum of £21,000 had been raised—the original estimated cost for a "plain building sufficient for the present needs of the School". Initially, eight Glaswegian architectural practices were invited to compete for the design of the building, including Honeyman & Keppie, although later this number was increased to twelve. The sum of £14,000 was put aside for the entire building costs, with the balance kept back to cover the assessors' fees, painting and the construction of a retaining wall. The committee decided that any firm whose plans exceeded this budget by more than ten per cent would be excluded from the competition. All the architects involved, however, were united in declaring that it would be impossible to provide all the accommodation requested for the sum agreed. Eventually, a compromise was reached and the various firms were requested to specify on their plans that portion of the building which could be built for £14,000 and to further submit an estimated cost for their entire schemes.

Gegen Ende des 19. Jahrhunderts stellte sich heraus, daß die Glasgow School of Art in ihren bisherigen Räumlichkeiten in den Corporation Galleries der wachsenden Zahl von Studenten nicht mehr genügend Platz bot. Daraufhin rief Francis H. Newbery, der Direktor der Schule, im September 1895 eine Versammlung des Schulbeirats ein, um über die Finanzierung eines Neubaus zu beratschlagen. Im Februar 1896 war der Betrag von 21000 Pfund aufgebracht— die ursprünglich geschätzten Kosten für ein „einfaches Gebäude, das den gegenwärtigen Anforderungen der Schule Genüge tut". Zunächst wurden acht Glasgower Architekturbüros—darunter Honeyman & Keppie—eingeladen, sich an dem Wettbewerb für den Neubau der Schule zu beteiligen; später wurde diese Zahl auf zwölf erweitert. Für die reinen Baukosten veranschlagte das Baukomitee die Summe von 14000 Pfund; von den restlichen 7000 Pfund sollten die Juryhonorare, der Anstrich und die Errichtung einer Stützmauer finanziert werden. Jeder Entwurf, dessen Kostenvoranschlag das Budget um mehr als zehn Prozent überschreiten würde, sollte vom Wettbewerb ausgeschlossen werden. Alle beteiligten Architekten erklärten jedoch einmütig, daß es unmöglich sei, den gestellten Anforderungen mit diesem Budget gerecht zu werden. Schließlich fand man einen Kompromiß: Die Architekten wurden gebeten, in ihren Bauplänen diejenigen Gebäudeteile zu spezifizieren, die das Limit von 14000 Pfund nicht überschritten. Zusätzlich wurden sie gebeten, einen Kostenvoranschlag für die geschätzten Gesamtkosten einzureichen.

Au tournant du siècle, les locaux de la Glasgow School of Art, alors situés dans les Corporation Galleries, ne suffisaient plus à accueillir l'afflux croissant des nouveaux étudiants. En septembre 1895, Francis H. Newbery, directeur de l'école, convoqua les administrateurs pour décider du lancement d'une souscription afin de construire un nouveau bâtiment. En 1896, quelque 21000 livres sterling avaient été réunies, ce qui correspondait au devis initial pour «un bâtiment simple convenant aux besoins actuels de l'école». Dans une première étape huit agences d'architecture de Glasgow, dont Honeyman & Keppie, furent appelées à concourir. Leur nombre passa plus tard à douze. La somme de 14000 livres sterling fut réservée aux coûts de construction, le solde devant couvrir les honoraires des membres du jury, la peinture et la construction d'un mur de soutènement. Le jury décida que toutes les agences dont le projet dépassera cette somme de plus de dix pour cent seraient immédiatement mises hors concours. Mais tous les architectes concernés déclarèrent qu'il était impossible de réaliser l'ensemble du programme avec un budget aussi modeste. On finit par trouver un compromis, aux termes duquel les différentes agences devaient préciser sur leurs plans ce qui pouvait être réalisé pour 14000 livres sterling, et fournir un devis pour le coût total du projet.

RIGHT PAGE | RECHTE SEITE | PAGE DE DROITE:
Main entrance on Renfrew Street, north façade
Haupteingang an der Renfrew Street, Nordfassade
Entrée principale, Renfrew Street, façade nord

TOP: General view from Renfrew Street
OBEN: Gesamtansicht von der Renfrew Street
CI-DESSUS: Vue générale depuis Renfrew Street

RIGHT: North elevation, 1910
RECHTS: Aufriß der Nordfassade
A DROITE: Elévation de la façade nord

RIGHT PAGE: West façade
RECHTE SEITE: Westfassade
PAGE DE DROITE: Façade ouest

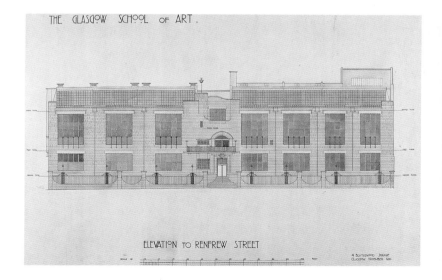

THE GLASGOW SCHOOL OF ART.

ELEVATION TO RENFREW STREET

GLASGOW SCHOOL OF ART, 167 RENFREW STREET, GLASGOW, 1897–1899 & 1907–1909

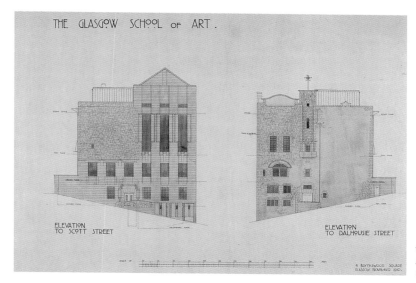

THE GLASGOW SCHOOL OF ART.

ELEVATION TO SCOTT STREET

ELEVATION TO DALHOUSIE STREET

West and east elevations, 1910
Aufriß der West- und Ostfassade
Elévation des façades ouest et est

On 13 January 1897, the Governors met to announce that Honeyman & Keppie had been awarded the commission. A month later, Mackintosh's plans for the new School were displayed at the Corporation Galleries amidst great controversy. It had been widely known that Newbery had insisted upon the selection of this building, which was regarded by many as a diverting exercise into the Art Nouveau style. Although the Memorial Stone was laid on 25 May 1898, construction work had already commenced in the last few months of 1897, since it had been decided that the foundations for the whole building should be laid. Built virtually to plan, the eastern section was opened in December 1899 and included the notable asymmetrical entrance that visually anchors the north elevation. The plans for the western half of the building were revised between September 1906 and May 1907. Construction began in 1907 and work was completed in 1909. The resulting west elevation reveals a maturity and an increasing confidence, as well as a full knowledge of the progressive developments in design and architecture that were occurring on the Continent. The most significant features of this magnificent elevation are the soaring library windows. Nikolaus Pevsner wrote in his book *Pioneers of Modern Design* (1975) of this façade, "Building in his [Mackintosh's] hands becomes an abstract art, both musical and mathematical. (...) Here the abstract artist is primarily concerned with the shaping of volume and not of space, of solids not voids."

Am 13. Januar 1897 gab der Schulbeirat bekannt, daß das Architekturbüro Honeyman & Keppie den Zuschlag für den Neubau der Glasgow School of Art erhalten habe. Im darauffolgenden Monat wurden Mackintoshs Pläne für die neue Schule in den Corporation Galleries öffentlich ausgelegt, was zu heftigen Kontroversen führte. Es war allgemein bekannt, daß Newbery auf Mackintoshs Entwurf bestanden hatte, den viele als eine mißglückte Übung im Jugendstil empfanden. Obwohl die offizielle Grundsteinlegung erst am 25. Mai 1898 stattfand, war bereits gegen Ende des Jahres 1897 mit den Bauarbeiten begonnen worden, nachdem entschieden worden war, das Fundament für das gesamte Gebäude zu legen. Der Ostteil der Schule mit seinem auffallend asymmetrischen Eingang, der die Ostfassade optisch an die Nordfassade anbindet, wurde im Dezember 1899 fertiggestellt. Die Pläne für den Westteil des Gebäudes wurden zwischen September 1906 und Mai 1907 nochmals überarbeitet; die Bauarbeiten begannen 1907 und waren 1909 vollendet. Die Westfassade offenbart nicht nur die Reife und das wachsende Selbstvertrauen des Architekten, sondern bezeugt überdies, daß er sich die Entwicklungen in der Formgebung und in der Architektur, die sich auf dem Kontinent vollzogen, zu eigen gemacht hatte. Das augenfälligste Merkmal der großartigen Fassade sind die hoch aufragenden Fenster der Bibliothek. Nikolaus Pevsner schrieb in seinem Buch *Pioneers of Modern Design* (1975) über diese Fassade: "Unter seinen [Mackintoshs] Händen wird Bauen zu einer abstrakten Kunst, ebenso von der Musik wie von der Mathematik bestimmt. (...) Der abstrakte Künstler befaßt sich hier vor allem mit der Gestaltung des Volumens, nicht des Raumes, mit der Gestaltung des Festen, nicht des Leeren."

Le 13 janvier 1897, le conseil d'administration annonça que la firme Honeyman & Keppie avait remporté le concours. Un mois plus tard, les plans de Mackintosh pour la nouvelle école, qui étaient exposés aux Corporation Galleries, suscitèrent une vive controverse. On savait que Newbery avait fortement pesé sur le choix du jury, et le projet lauréat était considéré par beaucoup comme un amusant exercice de style Art nouveau. La «première» pierre fut posée le 25 mai 1898, mais les travaux avaient commencé à la fin de 1897, avec la mise en place des fondations. La seconde tranche dut toutefois attendre une décennie. L'aile est de l'école fut ouverte en 1899. Construite presque exactement selon le projet, elle comprenait l'étonnante entrée asymétrique qui fournit à la façade nord son élément visuel principal. Les plans de la moitié ouest du bâtiment furent revus entre septembre 1906 et mai 1907. Les travaux commencèrent en 1907 et furent achevés en 1909. La nouvelle façade ouest révèle une maturité et une confiance accrues de la part de l'architecte. On peut y voir aussi sa familiarité avec l'évolution des arts appliqués et de l'architecture en Europe. Les baies vertigineuses de la bibliothèque sont le trait le plus saillant de cette magnifique façade, qu'évoque Nikolaus Pevsner dans *Pioneers of Modern Design* (1975): «Sous le crayon de Mackintosh, la construction tient à la fois de la musique et de la mathématique, et se transforme en art abstrait. (...) L'artiste abstrait s'intéresse davantage à la constitution du volume qu'à celle de l'espace, davantage aux pleins qu'aux vides.»

LEFT PAGE: East façade
LINKE SEITE: Ostfassade
PAGE DE GAUCHE: Façade est

TOP: Armchair designed for the director's room
OBEN: Armlehnstuhl, entworfen für das Direktorenzimmer
CI-DESSUS: Fauteuil conçu pour le bureau du directeur

RIGHT: The boardroom
RECHTS: Der Konferenzsaal
A DROITE: La salle du conseil

RIGHT: The library
RECHTS: Die Bibliothek
CI-CONTRE: La bibliothèque

FAR RIGHT: Design for the library
chandelier, 1909
RECHTS AUSSEN: Entwurfszeichnung für
die Bibliotheksleuchten
CI-CONTRE A DROITE: Projet d'éclairage
pour la bibliothèque

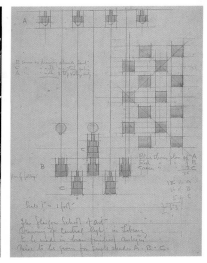

The double-height library interior is startlingly modern, with its screened gallery supported by vertical timbers which fluently divide the space and the floor-to-ceiling windows, allowing this dark, wood-panelled room to be bathed with light. The inherent richness of the library interior signifies its importance as the spiritual and intellectual heart of the building. Another important element of the second stage of building was the addition of an attic storey which incorporated a loggia, originally painted a warm terracotta colour, and a remarkable cantilevered glass and timber passageway that linked the two sides of the school. This glazed corridor projects just over two metres from the wall of the director's studio and is supported by load-bearing triangular iron brackets. The walkway was referred to by the students as the "Hen Run". This name was coined because the school was segregated by gender and this passageway was used by the female students to enter the male side of the building—"hen" being a Glasgewian colloquialism for "woman". The School of Art is indisput-ably Mackintosh's masterpiece, being not only his largest architectural project but also his most innovative. It has been more influential than any of his other buildings and has remained a place of pilgrimage for many subsequent generations of architects.

Die Innenraumgestaltung der zweigeschossigen Bibliothek wirkt erstaunlich modern mit ihrer von einer Brüstung eingefaßten Galerie, deren hölzerne Stützen den Raum teilen, und den vom Fußboden bis zur Decke reichenden Fenstern, die den dunkel getäfelten Raum in helles Licht tauchen. Die Sorgfalt, mit der die Bibliothek eingerichtet wurde, belegt ihre Bedeutung als sprirituelles und intellektuelles Zentrum der Schule. Weitere wichtige Elemente des zweiten Bauabschnitts waren das Attikageschoß mit einer ursprünglich in warmen Terrakottatönen gehaltenen Loggia und ein verglaster Verbindungsgang aus Holz, der die beiden Teile der Schule miteinander verbindet. Der verglaste Durchgang, der an der Rückseite des Direktorenzimmers liegt, ragt mehr als zwei Meter vor und wird von eisernen Dreieckskonsolen getragen. Er wurde von den Studenten „Hen Run" (Hühnerstieg, „Huhn" ist ein pejorativer Glasgower Ausdruck für Frau) genannt, weil die Studentinnen in der nach Geschlechtern getrennten Schule durch diesen Gang zur „männlichen" Seite gelangten. Die Glasgow School of Art ist zweifellos Mackintoshs Meisterwerk. Sie war nicht nur sein größtes Bauvorhaben, sondern auch sein innovativstes. Sie hat mehr Einfluß ausgeübt als jedes andere seiner Gebäude und ist bis heute ein Wallfahrtsort für Generationen von Architekten geblieben.

L'intérieur de la bibliothèque sur deux niveaux est lui aussi étonnamment moderne, avec sa galerie en mezzanine portée par des poteaux de bois qui scandent discrètement l'espace et avec ses fenêtres toute-hauteur qui inondent de lumière la salle de lecture lambrissée de bois foncé. La richesse de cet intérieur symbolise bien l'importance de la bibliothèque, cœur spirituel et intellectuel de l'institution. Autre élément important de la deuxième tranche: l'adjonction d'un attique doté d'une loggia—peinte à l'origine d'un rouge profond terre cuite—et d'un remarquable passage de verre et de bois en encorbellement reliant les deux ailes de l'école. Ce couloir vitré est en saillie de plus de deux mètres par rapport au mur du bureau du directeur et est porté par des consoles métalliques triangulaires. Les étudiants l'avaient surnommé «le poulailler» (par allusion aux «poules», autrement dit les jeunes filles dans l'argot de Glasgow). L'école n'étant pas mixte, les étudiantes devaient l'emprunter pour se rendre aux cours de dessin, dans la partie «Hommes». La Glasgow School of Art est sans conteste le chef-d'œuvre de Mackintosh. C'est son plus grand projet et le plus novateur. L'influence de ce bâtiment est sans équivalent et l'école est restée un lieu de pèlerinage pour des générations d'architectes.

RIGHT PAGE: The library
RECHTE SEITE: Die Bibliothek
PAGE DE DROITE: La bibliothèque

Interiors for Argyle Street Tea Rooms 1897–1898 & 1906

Armchair designed for the luncheon room
Armlehnstuhl, entworfen für den Speisesaal
Fauteuil conçu pour la salle à manger

As with the Buchanan Street Tea Rooms, Mackintosh and George Walton were both involved in the refurbishment of 114 Argyle Street. For this project, however, their roles were reversed, with Mackintosh designing all the required furniture and Walton, a bank clerk who had attended evening classes at the School of Art, executing several stencilled wall decorations. The furniture was of solid oak construction and remained in the tradition of the Arts & Crafts Movement, although it was less influenced by Charles F. A. Voysey than the earlier Gladsmuir designs which had been commissioned by William Davidson for his home near Kilmacolm. The smoking room at the Argyle Street Tea Rooms gave the impression of a countryside public house-cum-farmhouse parlour, with the dark and heavy furniture juxtaposed against Walton's delicate and lightly coloured wall stencils. Mackintosh also designed the famous high-backed chair with a pierced elliptical backrail for the luncheon room. The high back of these chairs not only provided a degree of privacy for the user but also aided in spatially dividing the long and narrow room. Mackintosh's final scheme for Argyle Street, the "Dutch Kitchen" of 1906, was defined by the *Architectural Review* magazine in 1935 as "the prototype of innumerable Miss Hook of Holland Cafes".

Wie schon bei den Buchanan Street Tea Rooms waren auch bei der Gestaltung der Tea Rooms in der Argyle Street 114 sowohl Mackintosh als auch George Walton beteiligt. Bei diesem Projekt arbeiteten sie jedoch mit vertauschten Rollen. Während Mackintosh für das gesamte Mobiliar verantwortlich war, entwarf Walton—ein ehemaliger Bankangestellter, der an der Glasgow School of Art Abendkurse besucht hatte—mehrere Schablonen-Wanddekors. Die aus massiver Eiche gefertigten Möbel von Mackintosh standen zwar noch ganz in der Tradition der Arts-and-Crafts-Bewegung, waren aber weniger stark von Charles F. A. Voysey beeinflußt als seine früheren Gladsmuir-Entwürfe, die William Davidson für sein Haus bei Kilmacolm in Auftrag gegeben hatte. Der Rauchsalon der Argyle Street Tea Rooms wirkte mit seinen dunklen, schweren Möbeln, die sich stark von Waltons zartem und hellem Wandschmuck absetzten, wie ein ländliches Pub oder eine Bauernstube. Für den Speisesaal entwarf Mackintosh seinen berühmten Stuhl mit hoher Rückenlehne und ovalem Kopfstück. Die hohen Rückenlehnen gaben den Gästen nicht nur ein Gefühl von Privatheit, sondern trugen auch dazu bei, den langen, engen Speisesaal harmonisch zu gliedern. Mackintoshs letzter Beitrag für die Argyle Street Tea Rooms, die „Holländische Küche" von 1906, wurde 1935 von der *Architectural Review* als „Prototyp zahlloser holländischer Kaffeehäuser" bezeichnet.

Comme dans le cas du Buchanan Street Tea Rooms, Mackintosh et George Walton participèrent tous les deux à la rénovation du 114 Argyle Street. Mais dans ce projet les rôles furent inversés, puisque Mackintosh réalisa tout le mobilier, tandis que Walton, employé de banque qui avait suivi les cours du soir à la Glasgow School of Art, exécuta plusieurs décorations au pochoir. Le mobilier était en chêne massif, dans la tradition du mouvement Arts & Crafts. Il est pourtant moins influencé par Charles F. A. Voysey que ne l'était le mobilier de Gladsmuir, commandé à Mackintosh pour la villa de William Davidson aux environs de Kilmacolm. Le fumoir du Argyle Street Tea Rooms rappelait l'atmosphère d'une salle d'auberge rustique, avec son mobilier sombre et massif contrastant avec les élégants pochoirs pastel de George Walton. Mackintosh dessina également pour la salle à manger la célèbre chaise à dossier haut percé d'une découpe en ellipse. Ce dossier permettait d'isoler les clients et de diviser l'espace de cette longue pièce étroite. En 1906, Mackintosh réalisa également pour Argyle Street la «Dutch Kitchen» (Cuisine hollandaise), qui fut qualifiée en 1935 par le magazine *Architectural Review* «de prototype d'innombrables cafés <Miss Hook of Holland>».

TOP: The luncheon room
OBEN: Der Speisesaal
CI-DESSUS: La salle à manger

LEFT: The billiard room
LINKS: Der Billardraum
A GAUCHE: La salle de billard

BOTTOM LEFT: The "Dutch Kitchen", 1906
LINKS UNTEN: Die „Holländische Küche"
CI-DESSOUS A GAUCHE: La «Cuisine hollandaise»

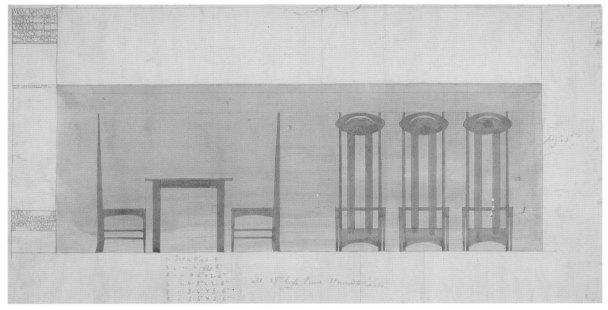

Furniture design for the luncheon room, 1897
Entwurfszeichnung für die Möblierung des Speisesaals
Projet de mobilier pour la salle à manger

Armchair designed for the smoking room and the billiard room
Armlehnstuhl, entworfen für den Rauchsalon und den Billardraum
Fauteuil conçu pour le fumoir et la salle de billard

The smoking room
Der Rauchsalon
Le fumoir

INTERIORS FOR ARGYLE STREET TEA ROOMS, 114 ARGYLE STREET, GLASGOW, 1897–1898 & 1906

High-backed chair designed for the luncheon room

Stuhl mit hoher Rückenlehne, entworfen für den Speisesaal

Chaise à haut dossier conçue pour la salle à manger

QUEEN'S CROSS CHURCH 1898

Roof trusses
Der Dachstuhl
La charpente du toit

Queen's Cross Church, formerly known as St. Matthew's Free Church, was designed by Mackintosh immediately after completing his entry for the School of Art competition. Queen's Cross Church is the only complete ecclesiastical building designed by Mackintosh, although he did produce a number of internal fittings for Holy Trinity, Bridge of Allan, and Abbey Close Church, Paisley, as well as submitting an entry to the Liverpool Anglican Cathedral competition of 1903. Construction of the church did not begin until June 1898 and it was eventually opened for public worship on 10 September 1899. Although constrained by a traditional form, Mackintosh's building is surprisingly modern in its use of huge exposed steel roof ties. It has been suggested that the unusual tower structure, which lends mass to the building, was inspired by a parish church at Merriot, near Crewkerne, Somerset, which Mackintosh had previously visited and sketched. The church imparts a sense of space and tranquillity, not an easy accomplishment given its awkward corner site on a busy crossroads in one of the poorest areas in Glasgow.

Die ursprünglich St. Matthew's Free Church genannte Queen's Cross Church entwarf Mackintosh unmittelbar nach Fertigstellung seines Wettbewerbsbeitrags für die Glasgow School of Art. Bei diesem Projekt handelt es sich um das einzige sakrale Bauwerk, das in seiner Gesamtheit von Mackintosh entworfen und auch realisiert wurde. In der Folgezeit schuf Mackintosh nur noch einzelne Inneneinrichtungselemente für die Holy Trinity Church in Bridge of Allan und die Abbey Close Church in Paisley. 1903 beteiligte er sich außerdem am Wettbewerb für die Anglican Cathedral in Liverpool. Die Bauarbeiten für die Queen's Cross Church begannen im Juni 1898; am 10. September 1899 konnte die Kirche geweiht werden. Trotz der Beschränkung auf weitgehend traditionelle Formen wirkt Mackintoshs Kirchenbau durch die Offenlegung der Dachkonstruktion überraschend modern. Man nimmt an, daß Mackintosh sich bei dem Entwurf des ungewöhnlichen Turms, der dem Gebäude Masse verleiht, von einer Pfarrkirche in Merriot bei Crewkerne in Somerset inspirieren ließ, die er früher einmal besucht und skizziert hatte. Obwohl sie an einer belebten Straßenkreuzung in einem der ärmsten Stadtviertel Glasgows liegt, vermittelt die Queen's Cross Church ein Gefühl von Weiträumigkeit und Ruhe.

Eglise connue antérieurement sous le nom de St. Matthew's Free Church, Queen's Cross Church fut conçue par Mackintosh immédiatement après qu'il eut remis son projet pour la Glasgow School of Art. L'église Queen's Cross est le seul édifice religieux conçu dans sa totalité par Mackintosh (à qui l'on doit toutefois les décorations intérieures de la Holy Trinity Church à Bridge of Allan et de l'Abbey Close Church à Paisley). Mackintosh a également participé au concours pour la cathédrale anglicane de Liverpool en 1903. La construction de Queen's Cross Church ne commença pas avant juin 1898, et elle fut ouverte au culte le 10 septembre 1899. Bien qu'il obéisse aux contraintes d'une forme traditionnelle, le bâtiment de Mackintosh est étonnamment moderne dans l'emploi de grandes traverses d'acier laissées apparentes. Le clocher assez surprenant, qui donne à l'église sa silhouette imposante, serait la réminiscence d'une église paroissiale de Merriot, près de Crewkerne dans le Somerset, que Mackintosh avait visitée et dessinée. Bien que située à un carrefour animé dans l'un des quartiers les plus pauvres de Glasgow, l'église dégage une impression d'espace et de tranquillité.

RIGHT PAGE: General view from Garscube Road
RECHTE SEITE: Gesamtansicht von der Garscube Road
PAGE DE DROITE: Vue générale depuis Garscube Road

INTERIORS FOR 120 MAINS STREET 1900

Detail of the dining-room
Detailansicht des Speisezimmers
La salle à manger, détail

Prior to his marriage to Margaret Macdonald in August 1900, Mackintosh internally redesigned and furnished a flat in Mains Street. The newlyweds moved into the apartment after their wedding and lived there until 1906, when they moved to 6 Florentine Terrace. The Mains Street interiors set an important precedent for Mackintosh's later domestic work—a light palette was used for the bedroom, drawing-room and studio while a darker colour scheme was adopted for the dining-room. The drawing-room fireplace is very similar in spirit to his Dunglass Castle fireplace of the same year, while the example in the studio is brutally simple and remarkably modern with its surround made up of fourteen roughly hewn six inch white boards. The lug chair, with a box-like construction and hidden foot-rest, functioned as a one-person fireside settle and contrasted strongly with the white furniture in the drawing-room.

Bevor Mackintosh im August 1900 Margaret Macdonald heiratete, entwarf er die Innenausstattung und das Mobiliar für eine Wohnung in der Glasgower Mains Street, die die Neuvermählten gleich nach ihrer Hochzeit bezogen. Hier wohnten sie bis 1906, als sie in die Florentine Terrace 6 umzogen. Die Einrichtung für die Wohnung in der Mains Street weist bereits eindeutig auf Mackintoshs spätere Arbeiten als Innenarchitekt voraus: Für das Schlafzimmer, das Wohnzimmer und das Atelier verwendete er helle Farben, während das Speisezimmer von dunkleren Tönen beherrscht wurde. Der Kamin im Wohnzimmer ähnelt formal dem des Dunglass Castle aus demselben Jahr, während der Kamin im Atelier mit seiner puristischen Verkleidung aus vierzehn roh bearbeiteten, weißen Sechs-Zoll-Brettern erstaunlich modern wirkt. Der Ohrensessel mit seiner kistenartigen Konstruktion und der verborgenen Fußstütze diente als abgeschirmter Ruheplatz vor dem Kamin und kontrastierte lebhaft mit den weißen Möbeln des Wohnzimmers.

Avant d'épouser Margaret Macdonald en août 1900, Mackintosh conçut la décoration intérieure et le mobilier d'un appartement à Mains Street. Les jeunes mariés s'y installèrent et y vécurent jusqu'en 1906, date à laquelle ils déménagèrent pour s'installer au 6 Florentine Terrace. Les intérieurs de Mains Street marquent une étape décisive dans le travail de décoration privée de Mackintosh: des couleurs très claires pour la chambre, le salon et l'atelier, une gamme de couleurs sombres pour la salle à manger. La cheminée du salon est très proche de celle de Dunglass Castle qui date de la même année. Celle de l'atelier est d'une simplicité brutale, et remarquablement moderne avec son encadrement de bois: quatorze planches de quinze centimètres grossièrement taillées et peintes en blanc. Le fauteuil à oreilles, conçu comme une boîte avec son repose-pieds caché, servait de siège de coin du feu pour une personne. Il contraste fortement avec le mobilier blanc du salon.

The drawing-room
Das Wohnzimmer
Le salon

The fireplace in the studio
Der Kamin im Atelier
La cheminée de l'atelier

TOP AND BOTTOM: The drawing-room
OBEN UND UNTEN: Das Wohnzimmer
CI-DESSUS ET CI-DESSOUS: Le salon

LEFT PAGE: High-backed chair designed for the drawing-room
LINKE SEITE: Stuhl mit hoher Rückenlehne, entworfen für das Wohnzimmer
PAGE DE GAUCHE: Chaise à haut dossier conçue pour le salon

Installation for the Eighth Secessionist Exhibition Vienna, 1900

LEFT: The Scottish Room
LINKS: Der Schottische Ausstellungsraum
A GAUCHE: La salle d'exposition écossaise

RIGHT PAGE | RECHTE SEITE | PAGE DE DROITE:
Margaret Macdonald-Mackintosh:
Embroidered textile panels, c. 1900
Bestickte Textilbanner
Panneaux brodés

In the autumn of 1900, the organizers of the Eighth Secessionist Exhibition—Koloman Moser, Josef Hoffman and the director of the Kunstgewerbeschule, Felician von Myrbach—invited The Four to contribute an interior to the exhibition, which was scheduled for the November of that year. For the Scottish Room, Mackintosh recreated a tea room interior in which the furniture was positioned against the walls. Apart from a large flower holder, which was arranged ikebana-style with wild flowers, the centre of the room remained bare. The extent of this room's influence can be seen in the later interiors by members of the Secession which were shown at the Tenth Secessionist Exhibition, and which were more sparsely furnished and significantly less cluttered than those examples from the Eighth Secessionist Exhibition. The art editor of the *Wiener Rundschau* journal wrote of the Scottish Room, "There is a Christlike mood in this interior (...) The decorative element is not proscribed, but is worked out with a spiritual appeal." Mackintosh designed all the furniture for this display, including a chair which was purchased by Koloman Moser and a smoking cabinet that was acquired by Josef Hoffmann's patron, Hugo Henneberg.

Im Herbst 1900 luden die Organisatoren der Achten Ausstellung der Wiener Sezession—Koloman Moser, Josef Hoffmann und der Direktor der Kunstgewerbeschule, Felician von Myrbach—die Glasgow Four ein, sich mit einer Raumgestaltung an der Ausstellung zu beteiligen, die im November desselben Jahres stattfinden sollte. Den Schottischen Ausstellungsraum gestaltete Mackintosh wie einen Teesalon. Sämtliche Möbel waren so an den Wänden aufgestellt, daß die Mitte des Raumes—abgesehen von einer großen Vase, in der im Ikebana-Stil arrangierte Feldblumen standen—leer blieb. Der nachhaltige Einfluß dieses Rau-mes auf die Mitglieder der Wiener Sezession zeigt sich in deren Inneneinrichtungen, die sie auf der Zehnten Sezessionsausstellung präsentierten: Verglichen mit der Achten Ausstellung waren die Interieurs weit sparsamer möbliert. Der Kunstkritiker der *Wiener Rundschau* schrieb über den Schottischen Ausstellungsraum, daß eine „christliche Stimmung" darin geherrscht habe. Das „dekorative Element" sei nicht verbannt, sondern herausgearbeitet und vergeistigt worden. Mackintosh entwarf das gesamte Mobiliar für den Ausstellungsraum, einschließlich eines Stuhls, den Koloman Moser kaufte, und eines Schranks für Rauchutensilien, den Hugo Henneberg, der Förderer Josef Hoffmanns, erwarb.

A l'automne 1900, les organisateurs de la Huitième Exposition de la Sécession viennoise (Koloman Moser, Josef Hoffmann et Felician von Myrbach, directeur de la Kunstgewerbeschule) invitèrent les Quatre de Glasgow à présenter un intérieur pour l'exposition prévue en novembre. Pour la «pièce écossaise», Mackintosh recréa un intérieur de salon de thé dans lequel le mobilier était placé contre le mur. A l'exception d'un grand vase qui contenait des fleurs sauvages disposées dans le style ikebana, le centre de la pièce demeurait vide. Cette pièce devait fortement influencer d'autres intérieurs par la suite, dont ceux des artistes de la Sécession exposés à la Dixième Exposition du mouvement viennois. Ces intérieurs étaient beaucoup moins meublés et nettement moins encombrés que ceux qui avaient été présentés à la Huitième Exposition. Le rédacteur artistique de la revue *Vienna Rundschau* devait écrire de la «pièce écossaise»: «Il règne dans cet intérieur une atmosphère quasi religieuse (...) L'élément décoratif n'est pas absent, mais il est traité de telle sorte qu'il fait naître un élan de spiritualité.» Mackintosh dessina tous les meubles exposés, y compris une chaise achetée par Koloman Moser et un cabinet à cigares, qui fut acquis par Hugo Henneberg, le mécène de Josef Hoffmann.

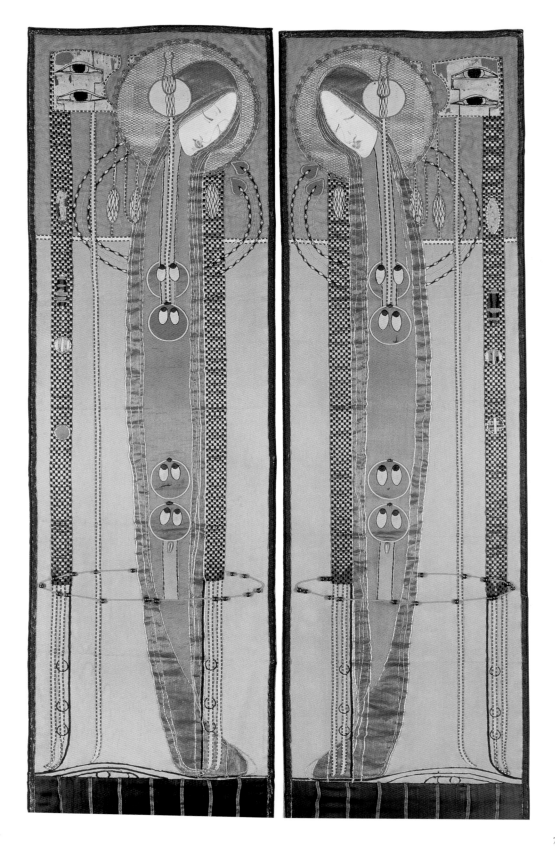

WINDYHILL
1900–1901

The dovecot
Der Taubenschlag
Le pigeonnier

Though smaller in scale, Windyhill is similar in plan to Hill House. Set on a hill, the house is approached from the north via a small courtyard with a fishpond in the centre—the whole effect of this entrance was intended to embrace the visitor. Unlike the later house, however, the service wing is visually dominated by the principal wing. With its grey harling (a rough-cast facing material), pitched roofs and severely plain south elevation, Windyhill embodies the character of a traditional Scottish farmhouse. Near the main entrance is a long horizontal window measuring over two metres in length, while the staircase bay, protruding from the rest of the house, also presages developments in architecture from the 1920's. Indeed, it could be claimed that the very modernity of these features is such that they work against the overall unity of design by contrasting too strongly with the vernacular spirit of the house.

Der Grundriß von Windyhill ähnelt stark dem des beträchtlich größeren Hill House. Von Norden kommend, gelangt man in das auf einem Hügel stehende Haus über einen kleinen Innenhof, in dessen Mitte ein Fischteich angelegt ist. Die Gestaltung der Eingangszone zielt darauf ab, den Besucher gleichsam in die Arme zu schließen. Im Gegensatz zum später erbauten Hill House wird bei Windyhill der Wirtschaftsflügel optisch vom Hauptflügel beherrscht. Mit seinem grauen Harling (einem schottischen Rauhputz), den hohen Giebeln und der strengen, schlicht gehaltenen Südfassade verkörpert Windyhill den Typus des traditionellen schottischen Landhauses. Neben dem Haupteingang befindet sich ein waagerechtes Fenster von mehr als zwei Meter Länge. Die abgerundete Außenmauer des Treppenhauses nimmt Entwicklungen in der Architektur vorweg, die erst in den 20er Jahren unseres Jahrhunderts voll zum Ausdruck gelangten. Es ließe sich einwenden, daß es gerade die Modernität dieser Details sei, die die Einheit des Ganzen störe, da sie zu stark mit dem traditionellen Charakter des Hauses kontrastiere.

Bien que plus modeste, la villa de Windyhill ressemble à Hill House par son plan. Elle est située sur une colline, et on y accède du côté nord après avoir traversé une petite cour avec un bassin au milieu: l'effet recherché était celui d'un resserrement de l'espace pour accueillir le visiteur. A la différence de Hill House, construite ultérieurement, l'aile des maîtres domine l'aile des services. Avec son revêtement gris de *harling* (sorte de crépi rugueux), ses toits pentus et sa façade sud plate et sévère, Windyhill a toutes les caractéristiques de la ferme écossaise traditionnelle. Près de l'entrée principale se trouve une grande fenêtre horizontale de plus de deux mètres de long. De la même façon la cage d'escalier en saillie sur la façade anticipe sur les développements architecturaux des années 20. On pourrait même dire que le fort contraste entre la modernité de la villa et son style vernaculaire gâche l'unité du projet.

Perspective drawing, 1900
Perspektivische Entwurfszeichnung
Dessin en perspective

General view from the north-east
Gesamtansicht von Nordosten
Vue générale du nord-est

Entrance hall
Die Eingangshalle
Le hall d'entrée

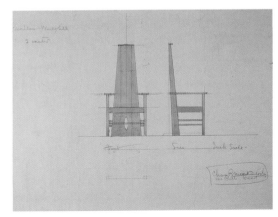

Design for the armchair, 1901
Entwurfszeichnung für den Armlehnstuhl
Projet de fauteuil

WINDYHILL, KILMACOLM, RENFREWSHIRE, 1900–1901

Armchair designed for the entrance hall
Armlehnstuhl, entworfen für die Eingangshalle
Fauteuil conçu pour le hall d'entrée

Reconstruction of the Chinese Room
Rekonstruktion des Chinesischen Raumes
Reconstruction du Salon chinois

INTERIORS FOR INGRAM STREET TEA ROOMS, INGRAM STREET, GLASGOW, 1900, 1907, 1909 & 1910–1911

Chair designed for the Oval Room and the ladies' rest room, 1909
Stuhl, entworfen für den ovalen Raum und die Damentoilette
Chaise conçue pour le Salon ovale et la salle de repos des dames

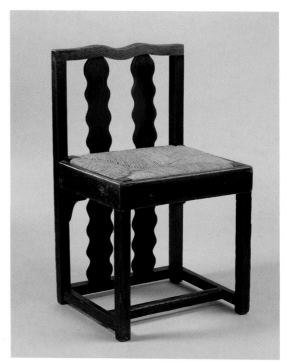

Chair designed for the Oak Room, 1907
Stuhl, entworfen für den Eichenraum
Chaise conçue pour le Salon en chêne

Barrel armchair, 1907
Armlehnstuhl in Faßform
Fauteuil cylindrique

Chair designed for the Chinese Room, 1911
Stuhl, entworfen für den Chinesischen Raum
Chaise conçue pour le Salon chinois

COMPETITION FOR THE HAUS EINES KUNSTFREUNDES 1901

Cover of the portfolio *Meister der Innenkunst*
Titelblatt der Mappe *Meister der Innenkunst*
Couverture du portfolio *Meister der Innenkunst*

In 1901, the *Zeitschrift für Innendekoration* launched a competition for the design and decoration of a "Haus eines Kunstfreundes" (House for an Art Lover). No first prize was awarded in the end, but Mackintosh received a special prize for his incorrectly submitted entry. The designs by Mackintosh, Mackay Hugh Baillie Scott and Leopold Bauer were considered to be the best three by the judges and were published, under the title *Meister der Innenkunst* (Masters of Interior Decoration), in portfolio form by Alexander Koch in 1902. For the competition, Hermann Muthesius wrote a précis on Mackintosh's design principles to accompany his series of plans and elevations. In this he noted: "The exterior architecture of the building evinces an absolutely original character, unlike anything else known. In it, we shall not find a trace of the conventional forms of architecture, to which the artist was quite indifferent." The interior decoration was restrained in colour and emphasised the textural qualities of the materials used. As a thoroughly modern and highly aesthetic dwelling for a connoisseur, Mackintosh's design amply fulfilled the competition's brief. The House for an Art Lover has recently been built in Glasgow's Bellahouston Park and houses the postgraduate department of the Glasgow School of Art.

Im Jahr 1901 schrieb die *Zeitschrift für Innendekoration* einen Ideenwettbewerb für den Entwurf und die Ausstattung des Hauses eines Kunstfreundes aus. Bei dem Wettbewerb wurde kein erster Preis vergeben. Mackintosh, der seinen Beitrag unvollständig eingereicht hatte, erhielt dennoch einen Sonderpreis. Die Entwürfe von Mackintosh, Mackay Hugh Baillie Scott und Leopold Bauer wurden von den Juroren als die drei besten bewertet und 1902 als Mappen unter dem Titel *Meister der Innenkunst* von Alexander Koch veröffentlicht. Hermann Muthesius stellte die abgebildeten Grund- und Aufrisse Mackintoshs mit einer Einführung vor, in der er die Kunstprinzipien Mackintoshs zusammenfaßte. Darin heißt es: „Das Äußere des Gebäudes ist ganz und gar einmalig, es gibt nichts, was ihm gleicht. Wir finden in dieser Architektur auch nicht die geringste Spur konventioneller Formen, denen gegenüber der Architekt momentan größte Gleichgültigkeit beweist." Die Inneneinrichtung war in den Farben verhalten und betonte die stofflichen Qualitäten der verwendeten Materialien. In seiner radikalen Modernität und kompromißlosen Ästhetik erfüllte Mackintoshs Entwurf die Bedingungen des Wettbewerbs wie kein anderer. Das „Haus eines Kunstfreundes" ist kürzlich im Glasgower Bellahouston Park gebaut worden und beherbergt das Post-Graduate Department der Glasgow School of Art.

En 1901, la revue *Zeitschrift für Innendekoration* lança un concours d'architecture et de décoration pour la «Haus eines Kunstfreundes» (Maison d'un amateur d'art). Le premier prix ne fut pas décerné, mais Mackintosh reçut une mention spéciale pour son projet hors concours. Les projets de Mackintosh, Mackay Hugh Baillie Scott et Leopold Bauer furent considérés comme les meilleurs par le jury et publiés en portfolio par Alexander Koch en 1902, sous le titre de *Meister der Innenkunst* (Les maîtres de la décoration intérieure). A l'occasion du concours, Hermann Muthesius rédigea un résumé des principes de composition de Mackintosh, pour accompagner la série de plans et de façades. Il notait ainsi: «L'architecture extérieure du bâtiment est d'une très grande originalité et foncièrement novatrice. On n'y trouvera aucune trace des formes conventionnelles de l'architecture, auxquelles l'artiste reste totalement indifférent». La palette de la décoration intérieure était sobre, pour mettre en valeur la texture des matériaux. Résolument moderne et esthétique, ce projet destiné à un connaisseur d'art remplissait pleinement les conditions du programme. La Maison d'un amateur d'art vient d'être construite—un siècle après—dans le parc Bellahouston de Glasgow. Elle doit recevoir les étudiants de dernière année de la Glasgow School of Art.

PAGES 88–89: Design for the music room
SEITEN 88–89: Entwurfszeichnung für das Musikzimmer
PAGES 88–89: Projet pour le salon de musique

TOP: Perspective drawing of the front façade
OBEN: Perspektivische Entwurfszeichnung der Frontfassade
CI-DESSUS: Dessin en perspective de la façade principale

BOTTOM: Reconstruction of the House for an Art Lover, Bellahouston Park, Glasgow
UNTEN: Rekonstruktion des Haus eines Kunstfreundes
CI-DESSOUS: Reconstruction de la Maison d'un amateur d'art

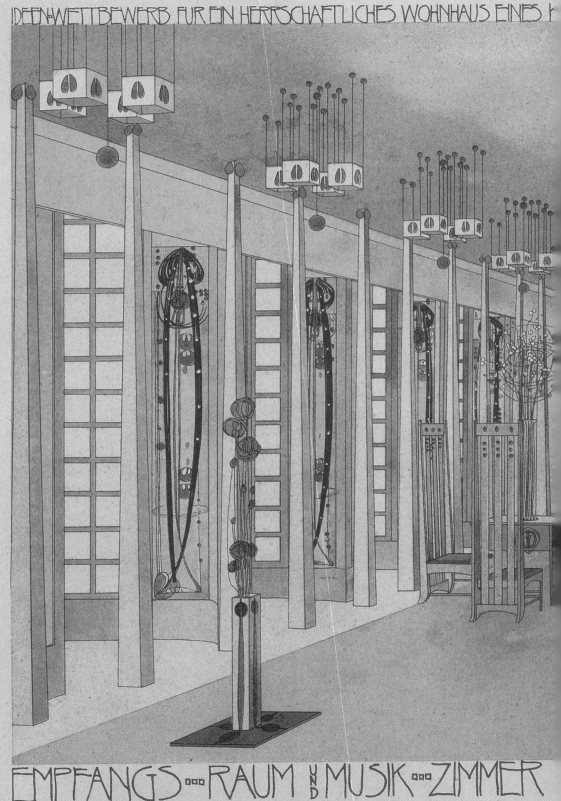

EMPFANGS-RAUM UND MUSIK-ZIMMER

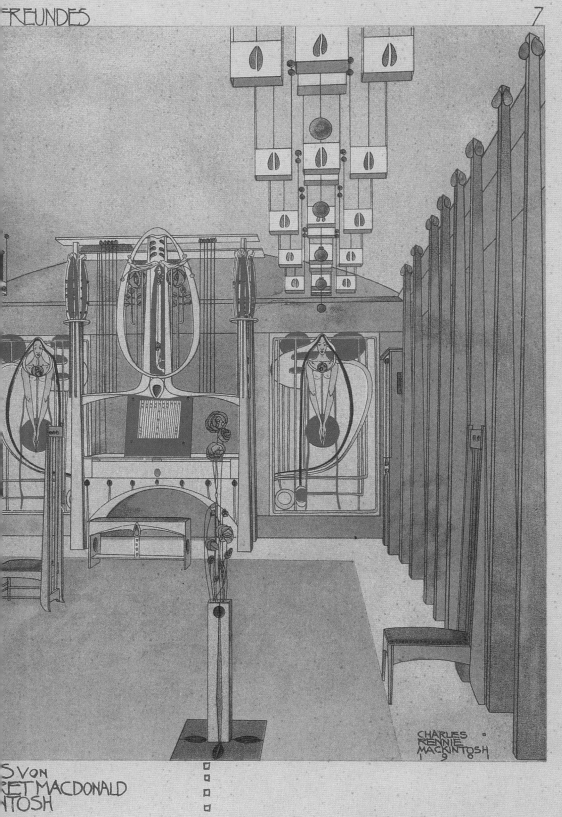

CHARLES
RENNIE
MACKINTOSH
1 9 0 1

C. R. MACKINTOSH. GLASGOW. HAUS EINES KUNST-FREUNDES.
VERLAGS-ANSTALT: ALEXANDER KOCH-DARMSTADT. — TAFEL VII.

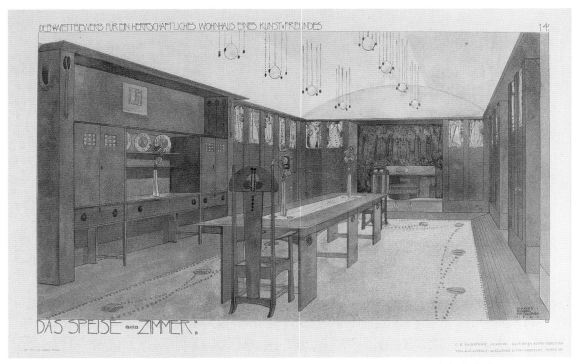

Design for the dining-room
Entwurfszeichnung für das Speisezimmer
Projet pour la salle à manger

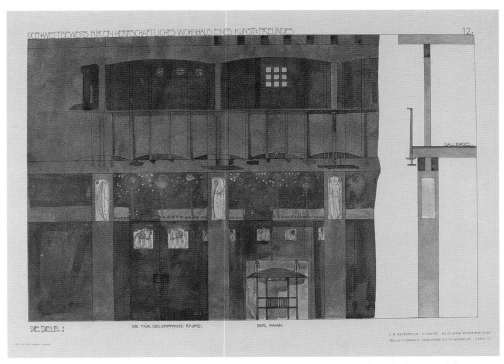

Design for the entrance hall
Entwurfszeichnung für die Eingangshalle
Projet pour le hall d'entrée

COMPETITION FOR THE HAUS EINES KUNSTFREUNDES, 1901

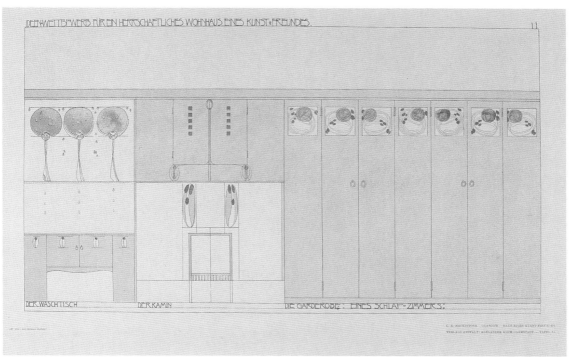

Design for the bedroom
Entwurfszeichnung für das Schlafzimmer
Projet pour la chambre à coucher

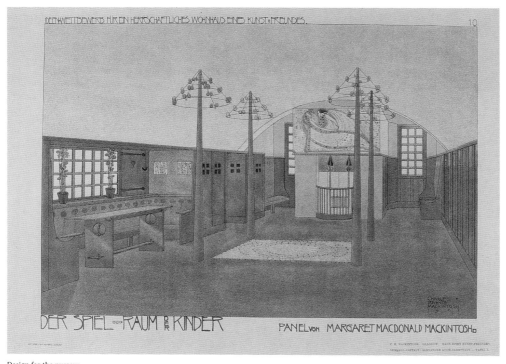

Design for the nursery
Entwurfszeichnung für das Kinderzimmer
Projet pour la nursery

INTERIORS FOR 14 KINGSBOROUGH GARDENS 1901–1902

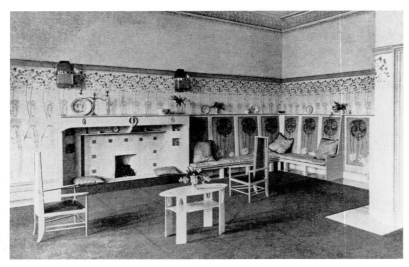

LEFT: The drawing-room
LINKS: Das Wohnzimmer
A GAUCHE: Le salon

RIGHT PAGE: Cabinet designed for the drawing-room
RECHTE SEITE: Schrank, entworfen für das Wohnzimmer
PAGE DE DROITE: Buffet conçu pour le salon

This terraced house (the address was later changed to 34 Kingsborough Gardens) belonged to Jessie Newbery's family, the Rowats, who commissioned Mackintosh to carry out internal renovations in late 1901. The femininity of the interiors designed for this project suggests the influence of Margaret Macdonald-Mackintosh. Writing on the delicacy of Mackintosh's white rooms, such as those at Kingsborough Gardens, Herman Muthesius commented in *Das Englische Haus* (1904): "Mackintosh's interiors achieve a level of sophistication which is way beyond the lives of even the artistically educated section of the population. The refinement and austerity of the artistic atmosphere prevailing here does not reflect the ordinariness that fills so much of our lives. (...) At least for the time being, it is hard to imagine that aesthetic culture will prevail so much in our lives that interiors like these will become commonplace. But they are paragons created by a genius, to show humanity that there is something higher in the distance which transcends everyday reality."

Dieses Reihenhaus (die jetzige Adresse ist Kingsborough Gardens 34) gehörte den Eltern von Jessie Newbery, den Rowats, die Mackintosh Ende 1901 damit beauftragten, die Inneneinrichtung zu renovieren. Der feminine Flair der daraus resultierenden Innenräume weist auf den Einfluß Margaret Macdonald-Mackintoshs hin. Hermann Muthesius sprach von der zarten Eleganz der weißen Räume Mackintoshs, wie sie auch hier zu finden ist. In *Das Englische Haus* (1904) schrieb er: „In Mackintoshs Räumen ist eine Verfeinerung ereicht, von deren Niveau selbst das Leben des künstlerisch gebildeten Teiles unseres Publikums noch weit entfernt ist. Die Feinheit und Strenge der hier waltenden künstlerischen Stimmung verträgt keine Einmischung des Gewöhnlichen, mit dem ja unser Leben gefüllt ist. (...) Es ist vorläufig nicht daran zu denken, daß unsere ästhetische Kultur so sehr das Übergewicht in unserem Leben haben wird, daß solche Räume allgemein werden. Aber sie sind Marksteine, die ein Genie weit hinausgeschoben hat, um der Menschheit das Höhere und Höchste in der Ferne vorzuzeichnen."

Cette maison en rangée, dont l'adresse devint par la suite 34 Kinsborough Gardens, appartenait à la famille de Jessie Newbery, les Rowat. Mackintosh fut chargé d'en réaliser la rénovation intérieure à la fin de 1901. Le côté féminin de la décoration de ce projet laisse deviner l'influence de Margaret Macdonald-Mackintosh. Hermann Muthesius commentera en ces termes la délicatesse des intérieurs blancs de Mackintosh, comme à Kinsborough Gardens, dans *Das Englische Haus* de 1904: «Les intérieurs de Mackintosh atteignent un niveau de sophistication qui dépasse largement le cadre de vie habituel des couches les plus cultivées et artistes de la société. L'atmosphère artistique, raffinée et austère qui y règne diffère radicalement de la banalité de nos vies quotidiennes. (...) Dans les conditions actuelles, on voit mal comment la culture visuelle pourrait faire des progrès tels que de semblables intérieurs puissent devenir courants. Mais ce sont des archétypes créés par un génie, qui servent à montrer à l'humanité qu'il existe quelque chose de plus noble et de plus élevé qui transcende le quotidien.»

Installation for the International Exhibition of Modern Decorative Art Turin, 1902

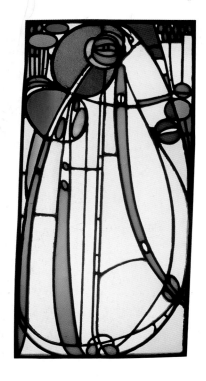

Glass panel designed for the Rose Boudoir
Bleiverglasung, entworfen für das „Rose Boudoir"
Vitrail conçu pour le «Rose Boudoir»

As director of the Glasgow School of Art, Francis H. Newbery received an invitation from the Organizing Committee of the International Exhibition of Modern Decorative Art to become a delegate for their Turin show of 1902, with the responsibility for selecting the Scottish exhibitors. Newbery viewed this as a perfect opportunity to display the talents of his Scottish students. When the Mackintoshes arrived at the exhibition and saw the unsympathetic nature of the space they were allocated, which consisted of three salons, they quickly made up enormous, column-like stencilled banners which acted as unifying features and also provided a powerful and theatrical entrance to the Scottish section. The first room was devoted to the Mackintoshes' Rose Boudoir, a feminine, dream-like interior of pink, silver and white. Described by the Austrian architect, Joseph Maria Olbrich, as "not (...) fully formed", this ethereal, sparsely furnished room was admonished by one critic of the time for having "the strangest mixture of puritanically severe functional forms and stylized subliminations of the practical". This type of interior led The Four to become known as the "Spook School".

In seiner Eigenschaft als Direktor der Glasgow School of Art erhielt Francis H. Newbery eine Einladung, als Delegierter an den Vorbereitungen der Internationalen Ausstellung für Moderne Dekorative Kunst von 1902 in Turin teilzunehmen. Seine Aufgabe bestand darin, schottische Designer und Innenarchitekten auszuwählen und diese um einen Beitrag für die Ausstellung zu bitten. Newbery sah darin eine ideale Möglichkeit, talentierte Studenten der Glasgow School of Art zu fördern. Als die Mackintoshs in Turin eintrafen und die ungünstigen Verhältnisse der ihnen zugewiesenen drei Ausstellungsräume sahen, fertigten sie riesige, säulenartige mit Schablonendekors verzierte Banner, die als eine Art Wegmarke dienten, und schufen so einen auffallenden, dekorativen Eingang für die Schottische Abteilung. Der erste Raum war dem „Rose Boudoir" der Mackintoshs gewidmet, einem sehr femininen, fast verträumt wirkenden Zimmer in Rosa, Silber und Weiß. Während der österreichische Architekt Joseph Maria Olbrich diesen ätherischen, spärlich möblierten Raum als „nicht (...) voll ausgeformt" bezeichnete, bemängelte ein zeitgenössischer Kritiker, daß er „eine seltsame Mischung puritanischer, funktionaler Formen und stilisierter Sublimationen des Praktischen" aufweise. Innenausstattungen wie die des „Rose Boudoir" trugen dazu bei, daß die Glasgow Four den Spitznamen der „Spook School" (Geisterschule) erhielten.

C'est en tant que directeur de la Glasgow School of Art que Francis H. Newbery fut invité par le comité d'organisation de l'Exposition internationale d'art décoratif moderne à participer à l'exposition de Turin de 1902. Il était chargé de la sélection des exposants écossais et cette occasion lui sembla idéale pour faire connaître le talent de ses étudiants. A leur arrivée à Turin, les Mackintosh trouvèrent peu engageant l'espace qui leur était alloué. Pour unifier leurs trois salons, ils conçurent sur le champ d'énormes draperies au pochoir, qui servaient en outre d'entrée théâtrale à la section écossaise. La première pièce était consacrée au «Rose Boudoir» des Mackintosh: un intérieur féminin de rêve, rose, argent et blanc. L'architecte autrichien Joseph Maria Olbrich estima que cet intérieur était «inachevé». Un autre critique de l'époque reprocha à cette pièce éthérée et à peine meublée d'être «un mélange surprenant de formes fonctionnelles, sévères et puritaines, et de fantasmes stylisés de la vie courante». C'est à des intérieurs de ce genre que les Quatre de Glasgow doivent leur surnom de «Spook School» (Ecole des Ectoplasmes).

RIGHT PAGE: Stencilled banners at the entrance to the Scottish section

RECHTE SEITE: Mit Schablonendekors verzierte Banner am Eingang der Schottischen Abteilung

PAGE DE DROITE: Draperies au pochoir à l'entrée de la section écossaise

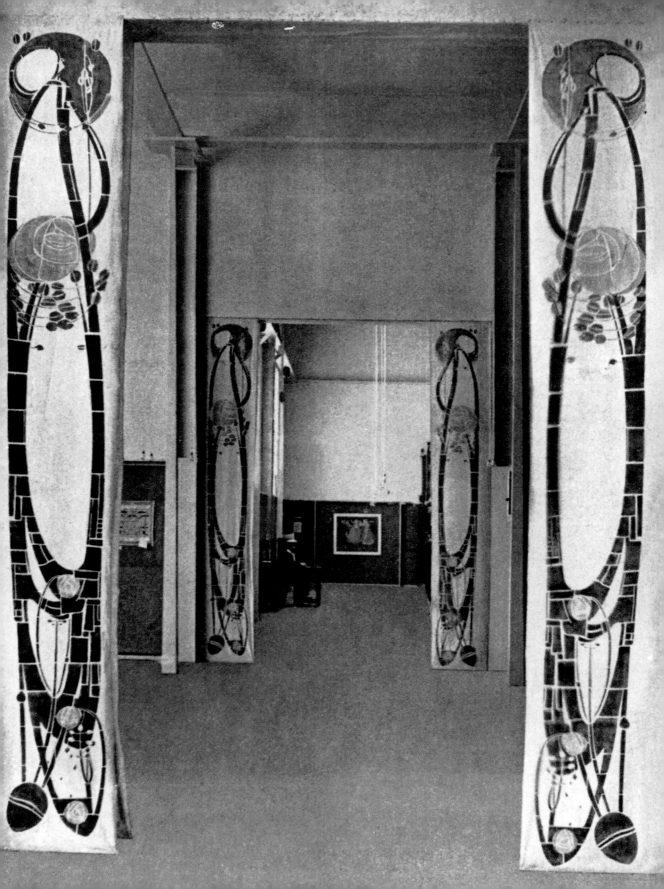

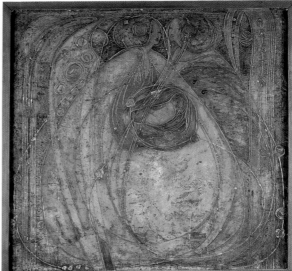

TOP | OBEN | CI-DESSUS:

Margaret Macdonald-Mackintosh:

The White Rose and the Red Rose | The Heart of the Rose, 1902
These two gesso panels hung opposite each other on the far walls of the
Rose Boudoir

Die weiße Rose und die rote Rose | Das Herz der Rose
Diese beiden bemalten Gipstafeln hingen einander gegenüber an den
Schmalseiten des „Rose Boudoir"

La Rose Blanche et la Rose Rouge | Le Cœur de la Rose
Ces deux panneaux en plâtre peint sont disposés face à face aux deux
extrémités du «Rose Boudoir»

RIGHT: The Rose Boudoir

RECHTS: Das „Rose Boudoir"

A DROITE: Le «Rose Boudoir»

RIGHT PAGE: High-backed chair with stencilled decorations
designed for the Rose Boudoir

RECHTE SEITE: Stuhl mit hoher Rückenlehne und Schablonendekor,
entworfen für das „Rose Boudoir"

PAGE DE DROITE: Chaise à haut dossier décoré au pochoir,
conçue pour le «Rose Boudoir»

INSTALLATION FOR THE INTERNATIONAL EXHIBITION OF MODERN DECORATIVE ART, TURIN, 1902

HILL HOUSE
1902–1903

Detail of the wrought-iron entrance gates
Detail des schmiedeeisernen Eingangstores
La grille d'entrée en fer forgé, détail

RIGHT PAGE: Entrance with wrought-iron gates
RECHTE SEITE: Eingang mit schmiedeeisernem Tor
PAGE DE DROITE: Entrée avec la grille en fer forgé

Hill House was the largest and most finely detailed of all Mackintosh's domestic buildings. It is also the only house designed by him to have retained its original interior. Hill House was Mackintosh's third large domestic building, having already assisted John Keppie with Redlands around 1899 and having independently designed Windyhill for William Davidson Jr. in 1900. In 1902, Talwin Morris recommended Mackintosh to Walter Blackie as a suitable architect for the publisher's new home. After viewing Windyhill, Blackie commissioned him to design a house in Helensburgh overlooking the Firth of Clyde. While Hill House shares many of the characteristics of Mackintosh's 1901 "Haus eines Kunstfreundes" design, it is less international and more Scottish in spirit. The exterior elevations of Hill House were dictated by the plans for the interior, a way of working that was quite radical at a time when most architects designed exteriors first and then attempted to fit in the necessary internal requirements. Even so, Mackintosh also paid a great deal of attention to every detail of the project, including, among many other innovative considerations, specially designed cupboards to meet the needs of the domestic staff, and planning the drawing-room in such way that its character would change with the seasons.

Das Hill House ist nicht nur das größte, sondern auch das am sorgfältigsten durchgeplante Wohnhaus, das Mackintosh je geschaffen hat. Zudem ist es das einzige, das noch die ursprüngliche, von Mackintosh entworfene Inneneinrichtung aufweist. Nach dem um 1899 zusammen mit John Keppie verwirklichten Redlands-Projekt und dem ausschließlich nach eigenen Plänen 1900 für William Davidson jr. gebauten Haus Windyhill war Hill House Mackintoshs drittes größeres Wohnhausprojekt. Als der Verleger Walter Blackie 1902 einen Architekten suchte, empfahl Talwin Morris ihm Mackintosh, und nach einer Besichtigung Windyhills erteilte er ihm den Auftrag, in Helensburgh ein Herrenhaus mit Blick auf den Firth of Clyde zu entwerfen. Das Hill House weist viele der charakteristischen Merkmale auf, die die Entwürfe für das Haus eines Kunstfreundes auszeichnen, doch ist es in seinem Erscheinungsbild stärker an schottischen Vorbildern orientiert. Die äusseren Umrisse des Hauses wurden von den Plänen für das Innere bestimmt—eine Vorgehensweise, die recht revolutionär war zu einer Zeit, da die meisten Architekten zunächst die Außenfassaden entwarfen und erst dann versuchten, die Raumaufteilung im Inneren dem äußeren Rahmen anzupassen. Mackintosh achtete auf jedes Detail des Projekts; so ließ er—neben vielen anderen Neuerungen—eigens für die Bedürfnisse des Personals entworfene Schränke anfertigen und gestaltete das Wohnzimmer so, daß es seinen Charakter mit dem Wechsel der Jahreszeiten veränderte.

C'est la plus grande et la plus raffinée des villas de Mackintosh. C'est aussi la seule qui ait conservé sa décoration d'origine. Hill House est la troisième villa de Mackintosh qui avait déjà participé avec Keppie à la construction de la villa Redlands vers 1899, et construit seul Windyhill pour William Davidson jr. en 1900. En 1902, Talwin Morris recommanda Mackintosh à Walter Blackie, qui songeait à se faire construire une nouvelle maison. Après avoir vu Windyhill, Blackie confia donc à Mackintosh la réalisation d'une villa à Helensburgh, avec vue sur le Firth of Clyde. Hill House ressemble par bien des aspects au projet «Haus eines Kunstfreundes» de 1901, mais elle est d'un style beaucoup plus écossais et moins international. A Hill House, ce sont les plans qui déterminent la façade, une méthode tout à fait radicale à l'époque, puisque la plupart des architectes dessinaient d'abord l'extérieur, avant d'y faire rentrer tant bien que mal les espaces intérieurs. Il n'en reste pas moins que Mackintosh accorda une importance particulière aux détails. Entre autres innovations on trouve des placards spécialement conçus pour faciliter le service des domestiques et l'organisation du salon de façon à profiter au mieux de chaque saison.

PAGES 104–105: General view from the south-east
SEITEN 104–105: Gesamtansicht von Südosten
PAGES 104–105: Vue générale du sud-est

TOP: Perspective drawing of the north façade
OBEN: Perspektivische Entwurfszeichnung der Nordfassade
CI-DESSUS: Dessin en perspective de la façade nord

BOTTOM: Perspective drawing of the south façade
UNTEN: Perspektivische Entwurfszeichnung der Südfassade
CI-DESSOUS: Dessin en perspective de la façade sud

LEFT PAGE: View from the east
LINKE SEITE: Ansicht von Osten
PAGE DE GAUCHE: Vue de l'est

TOP: The drawing-room
OBEN: Das Wohnzimmer
CI-DESSUS: Le salon

RIGHT: The fireplace in the drawing-room
RECHTS: Der Kamin im Wohnzimmer
A DROITE: La cheminée du salon

RIGHT PAGE: The entrance hall
RECHTE SEITE: Die Diele
PAGE DE DROITE: Le vestibule

HILL HOUSE, HELENSBURGH, DUNBARTONSHIRE, 1902–1903

The master bedroom, bed wall
Das herrschaftliche Schlafzimmer, Bettseite
La chambre à coucher principale, tête de lit

The master bedroom
Das herrschaftliche Schlafzimmer
La chambre à coucher principale

HILL HOUSE, HELENSBURGH, DUNBARTONSHIRE, 1902–1903

The master bedroom, fireplace wall

Das herrschaftliche Schlafzimmer, Kaminseite

Chambre à coucher principale, côté cheminée

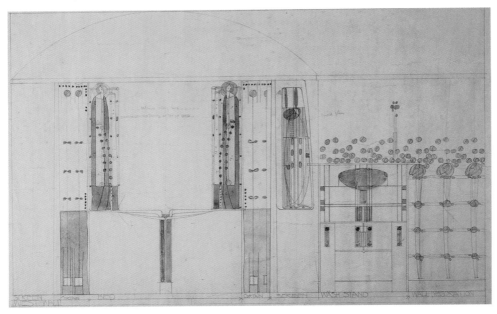

Design for the master bedroom, 1903

Entwurfszeichnung für das herrschaftliche Schlafzimmer

Projet pour la chambre à coucher principale

WILLOW TEA ROOMS
1903–1904 & 1917

Detail of the façade with exterior sign
Fassadendetail mit Geschäftsschild
La façade avec enseigne commerciale, détail

Opened to the public in October 1904, the design of the Willow Tea Rooms was the most coherently unified of the four tea rooms operated by Catherine Cranston. The site in Sauchiehall Street had been acquired in 1901, but Mackintosh, as sole designer of the project, did not begin the design for the building and its internal decorations until the Spring of 1903. Sauchiehall translates to "alley of the willows" and throughout this suite of rooms Mackintosh applied willow motifs both representationally and symbolically. Although generally very similar in layout to the Buchanan Street premises, the Willow Tea Rooms had an additional dining-room to the rear of the ground floor (the back saloon). This single-storey room, which measured some five and a half metres in height, facilitated the introduction of a galleried area. The steel roof trusses of this impressively lofty space were concealed by Mackintosh with a semi-open square framework timber ceiling which gave the interior a somewhat Japanese flavour.

Die Willow Tea Rooms, die im Oktober 1904 eröffnet wurden, waren von der Konzeption her der einheitlichste der vier von Catherine Cranston betriebenen Teesalons. Das Grundstück in der Sauchiehall Street hatte sie bereits 1901 erworben, aber Mackintosh, der alleinige Designer des Projekts, begann erst im Frühling des Jahres 1903 mit den Entwürfen für das Gebäude und die Inneneinrichtung. Die Übersetzung des gälischen Wortes Sauchiehall bedeutet „Allee der Trauerweiden", und Mackintosh verwendete das Motiv der Weide sowohl als realistische wie als symbolisch überhöhte Metapher in allen Räumen. Die Willow Tea Rooms wiesen einen ähnlichen Grundriß auf wie die der Buchanan Street, zusätzlich gab es an der Rückseite des Erdgeschosses einen Speisesaal. Dieser eingeschossige Anbau mit einer Höhe von fünfeinhalb Metern ermöglichte den Einbau einer Galerie. Mackintosh verbarg den stählernen Dachstuhl des ungewöhnlich hohen Raumes hinter einer halb geschlossenen, quadratisch getäfelten Holzdecke, die dem Saal eine japanische Note verlieh.

Ouvert au public en octobre 1904, ce salon de thé est le projet le plus cohérent des quatre établissements dirigés par Miss Cranston. La parcelle de Sauchiehall Street avait été achetée dès 1901, mais Mackintosh, seul responsable du projet, ne commença la conception du bâtiment et de sa décoration intérieure qu'au printemps 1903. Sauchiehall signifie «allée des saules», et dans toute la série de salons, Mackintosh a disposé des motifs de saule, tantôt purement figuratifs, tantôt traités dans la veine symboliste. Bien que très semblable aux locaux de Buchanan Street par son agencement, le Willow Tea Rooms avait une salle à manger supplémentaire à l'arrière du rez-de-chaussée. Cette pièce à un seul niveau avait une hauteur sous plafond de cinq mètres et demi permettant l'aménagement d'une mezzanine. Les fermes métalliques de la charpente sont dissimulées derrière un quadrillage de bois formant un faux plafond à claire-voie qui ajoute à ce lieu une note japonaise.

RIGHT PAGE: Front façade seen from Sauchiehall Street, c. 1904

RECHTE SEITE: Frontfassade, Blick von der Sauchiehall Street

PAGE DE DROITE: Façade principale, vue depuis Sauchiehall Street

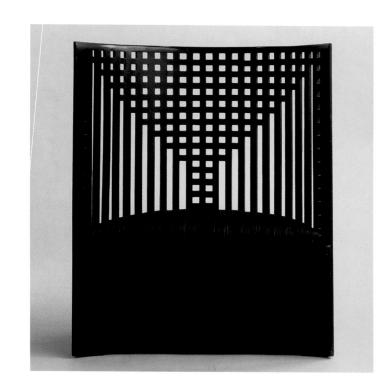

TOP: Pair of armchairs designed for the front saloon on the ground floor, the gallery and the smoking room

OBEN: Ein Paar Armlehnstühle, entworfen für den vorderen Salon im Erdgeschoß, die Galerie und den Rauchsalon

CI-DESSUS: Ensemble de deux fauteuils conçus pour le salon du rez-de-chaussée, la galerie et le fumoir

RIGHT: Curved lattice-back chair designed for the saloons on the ground floor

RECHTS: Stuhl mit gewölbter Gitter-Rückenlehne, entworfen für die Salons im Erdgeschoß

A DROITE: Chaise à dossier cintré en treillis, conçue pour les salons du rez-de-chaussée

RIGHT PAGE: View of the front saloon and the gallery above

RECHTE SEITE: Blick in den vorderen Salon und auf die Galerie

PAGE DE DROITE: Vue du salon avant et de la galerie

TOP: View of the gallery
OBEN: Blick auf die Galerie
CI-DESSUS: Vue de la galerie

RIGHT: View of the front saloon on the
ground floor
RECHTS: Blick in den vorderen Salon im
Erdgeschoß
A DROITE: Vue du salon avant du rez-de-chaussée

RIGHT PAGE: Pair of ladder-backed chairs designed
for the saloons on the ground floor and the gallery
RECHTE SEITE: Ein Paar Stühle mit Leiterrücken-
lehnen, entworfen für die Salons im Erdgeschoß und
die Galerie
PAGE DE DROITE: Ensemble de deux chaises-
échelles conçues pour les salons du rez-de-chaussée
et la galerie

WILLOW TEA ROOMS, 199 SAUCHIEHALL STREET, GLASGOW, 1903–1904 & 1917

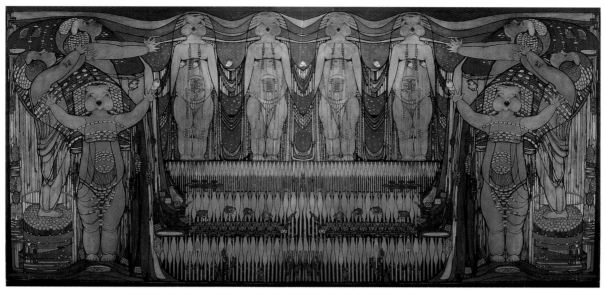

Margaret Macdonald-Mackintosh:

The Little Hills, c. 1915
Two canvases, oil on canvas, each 153.5 x 151 cm

Die kleinen Hügel
Zwei Leinwände, Öl auf Leinwand, je 153,5 x 151 cm

Les petites collines
Deux toiles, huile sur toile, chacune 153,5 x 151 cm

Around 1917, Catherine Cranston asked Mackintosh, who was now living in London, to create another tea room in the basement. His final Glaswegian commission, "The Dug-Out" had a wartime theme; windowless and with shiny black-leaded walls and ceilings, the interior must have been strongly reminiscent of a subterranean bunker. The darkness of this space was alleviated by canary-yellow settles and bold stencilled geometric decoration in emerald green and royal blue. Two other colourful elements which were introduced to "The Dug-Out" were the memorial fireplace depicting the flags of the allied nations and a pair of large-scale canvases, painted in oil by Margaret Macdonald-Mackintosh titled *The Little Hills*. They were inspired by Psalm 65, which optimistically ends: "The grasslands of the desert overflow; the hills are clothed with gladness. The meadows are covered with flocks and the valleys are mantled with corn; they shout for joy and sing."

Um 1917 bat Catherine Cranston Mackintosh, der mittlerweile in London lebte, im Kellergeschoß einen weiteren Teesalon einzurichten. Bei seinem letzten Glasgower Auftrag, dem „Dug-Out"-Raum (Unterstand) nahm sich Mackintosh thematisch des Krieges an: Die graphitgeschwärzten Wände des fensterlosen Raums erinnerten an einen unterirdischen Bunker. Die kanariengelben Sitzbänke und geometrischen Schablonendekors in Smaragdgrün und Königsblau schwächten die Dunkelheit des Salons jedoch ab. Zwei weitere Elemente, die dem „Dug-Out"-Raum Farbe verliehen, waren ein als Mahnmal dienender Kamin mit den Fahnen der Alliierten und zwei große Ölgemälde von Margaret Macdonald-Mackintosh mit dem Titel *Die kleinen Hügel*. Sie waren inspiriert vom 65. Psalm, der mit den euphorischen Worten endet: „Es triefen die Anger der Steppe, und mit Jubel gürten sich die Hügel; die Berge bekleiden sich mit Herden, und die Täler hüllen sich in Korn, jauchzen sich zu und singen."

Vers 1917, Miss Cranston demanda à Mackintosh, alors installé à Londres, de créer un nouveau salon de thé au sous-sol. Ce fut sa dernière commande à Glasgow. Appelée «The Dug-Out» (L'Abri), cette salle avait des connotations guerrières: aveugle, avec ses murs et son plafond entièrement peints en gris sombre, ce salon de thé évoquait irrésistiblement un bunker. Des canapés jaune canari et d'audacieux motifs géométriques vert émeraude et bleu roi, réalisés au pochoir, venaient égayer la relative obscurité du lieu. Le manteau de cheminée commémoratif représentant tous les drapeaux des nations alliées, et deux grandes huiles de Margaret Macdonald-Mackintosh intitulées *Les petites collines* mettaient également quelques taches de couleur. Ces toiles s'inspiraient de la conclusion optimiste du Psaume 65: «Les pâturages du désert regorgent d'eau; les collines sont pleines de joie; les prairies sont couvertes de troupeaux, et les vallées couvertes d'un manteau de blé; elles chantent un hymne à la joie.»

Design for "The Dug-Out", 1917
Entwurfszeichnung für den „Dug-Out"-Raum
Projet pour «L'Abri»

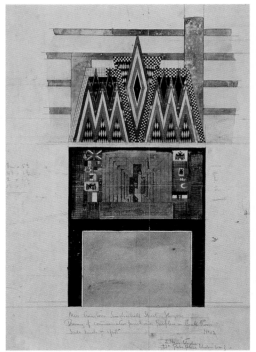

Design for the memorial fireplace in "The Dug-Out", 1917
Entwurfszeichnung für den Gedenkkamin im „Dug-Out"-Raum
Projet de cheminée commémorative dans «L'Abri»

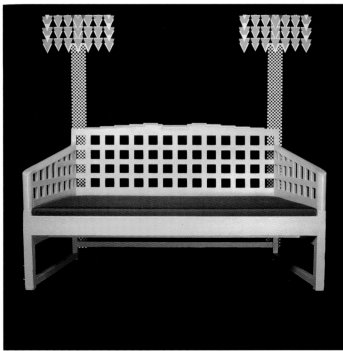

Settle designed for "The Dug-Out", 1917
Bank, entworfen für den „Dug-Out"-Raum
Canapé conçu pour «L'Abri»

INTERIORS FOR HOUS'HILL 1903–1905

Chair designed for the drawing-room
Stuhl, entworfen für das Wohnzimmer
Chaise conçue pour le salon

Around 1903, the tea room proprietress, Catherine Cranston, and her husband, Major John Cochrane, asked Mackintosh to redesign the interior of their home, Hous'hill. Mackintosh was granted an even greater creative freedom than at Hill House, having certainly designed more site-specific furniture for this project. Of special interest was a curved open-work screen that divided the drawing-room into a circular music room and a fireside area—a similar, though solid screen was used later in 1930 by the architect Ludwig Mies van der Rohe to define the dining area at the Tugendhat House in Brno. The geometric formality of the white bedroom at Hous'hill links it more closely to the installation for the Dresdener Werkstätten exhibition than to the bedroom at Hill House with its more naturalistic motifs. The blue bedroom was a radical stylistic departure for Mackintosh: all the furniture was rigidly geometric and either stained or ebonized. In 1909 he also designed a card room for Hous'hill, but unfortunately no photographs exist of this later project. Catherine Cranston left the house in around 1920 and it was destroyed by fire soon after.

Um 1903 beauftragten Catherine Cranston, die Inhaberin der Glasgower Teesalons, und ihr Ehemann, Major John Cochrane, Mackintosh, die Inneneinrichtung ihres Landhauses Hous'hill komplett neu zu gestalten. Sie räumten ihm dabei größere künstlerische Freiheiten ein, als er sie beim Bau des Hill House gehabt hatte, was sich auch in der weit höheren Anzahl von Möbeln äußert, die er speziell für dieses Projekt entwarf. Von besonderem Reiz war eine halbrunde, offen gearbeitete Stellwand, die das Wohnzimmer in ein rundes Musikzimmer und einen Kaminbereich teilte. Eine ähnliche, aber massiv gearbeitete Stellwand verwendete der Architekt Ludwig Mies van der Rohe im Jahre 1930, um den Eßbereich im Tugendhat-Haus in Brno abzutrennen. Die geometrische Formgebung des weißen Schlafzimmers im Hous'hill ähnelt formal weit mehr dem für die Dresdener Ausstellung gestalteten Ausstellungsraum als dem Schlafzimmer des Hill House mit seinen eher naturalistischen Motiven. Das blaue Schlafzimmer mit seinen dunkel gebeizten, streng geometrischen Möbeln bezeichnet dagegen einen stilistischen Wendepunkt im Werk Mackintoshs. Im Jahr 1909 entwarf er für Hous'hill noch ein Gesellschaftszimmer, von dem jedoch leider keine Fotografien erhalten sind. Um 1920 zog Catherine Cranston aus; das Haus fiel wenig später einem Feuer zum Opfer.

Aux environs de 1903, Catherine Cranston, propriétaire des salons de thé qui portaient son nom, et son mari le Major John Cochrane, demandèrent à Mackintosh de rénover l'intérieur de leur villa Hous'hill. La liberté de création de Mackintosh fut encore plus grande qu'à Hill House, et il conçut pour Hous'hill un mobilier encore plus spécifique. On remarquera tout particulièrement un écran circulaire à claire-voie, qui permettait de diviser le salon en coin du feu et salon de musique. Trente ans plus tard, Ludwig Mies van der Rohe devait utiliser un écran du même type, mais plein, pour délimiter le coin salle à manger de la villa Tugendhat de Brno. Le côté formel et géométrique de la chambre blanche de Hous'hill renvoie davantage à l'aménagement du Dresdener Werkstätten qu'à celle de Hill House, dont les motifs sont plus naturalistes. La chambre bleue marque un tournant important dans l'œuvre de Mackintosh: tous les meubles ont des formes géométriques rigides, et sont soit teintés dans la masse, soit peints couleur ébène. En 1909, il conçut également un salon de jeux pour Hous'hill. Il ne reste malheureusement aucune photo de ce projet tardif. Catherine Cranston déménagea en 1920, et la villa fut détruite peu après par un incendie.

The drawing-room
Das Wohnzimmer
Le salon

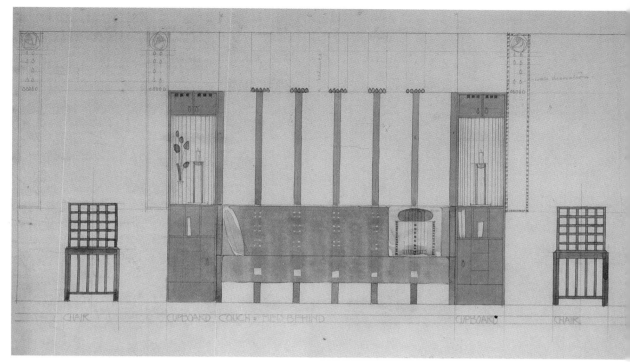

Design for the blue bedroom, 1904
Entwurfszeichnung für das blaue Schlafzimmer
Projet pour la chambre bleue

The blue bedroom
Das blaue Schlafzimmer
La chambre bleue

INTERIORS FOR HOUS'HILL, NITSHILL, GLASGOW, 1903–1905

Writing-desk designed for the blue bedroom
Sekretär, entworfen für das blaue Schlafzimmer
Secrétaire conçu pour la chambre bleue

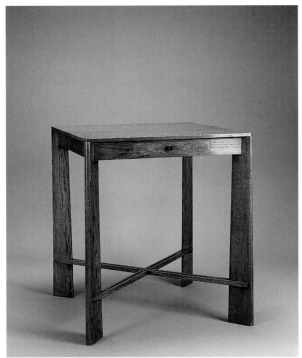

Square table designed for the blue bedroom
Quadratischer Tisch, entworfen für das blaue Schlafzimmer
Table carrée conçue pour la chambre bleue

Pen box designed for the white bedroom

Kästchen für Schreibutensilien, entworfen für das weiße Schlafzimmer

Plumier conçu pour la chambre blanche

Pair of candlesticks designed for the white bedroom

Ein Paar Kerzenhalter, entworfen für das weiße Schlafzimmer

Paire de chandeliers conçus pour la chambre blanche

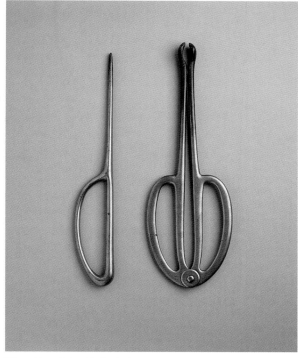

Poker and tongs designed for the drawing-room

Feuerhaken und -zange, entworfen für das Wohnzimmer

Tisonnier et pincettes conçus pour le salon

INTERIORS FOR HOUS'HILL, NITSHILL, GLASGOW, 1903–1905

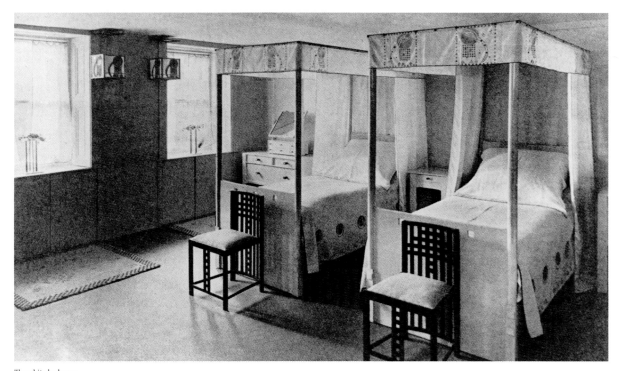

The white bedroom
Das weiße Schlafzimmer
La chambre blanche

Design for the stencilled decoration of the entrance hall, 1904
Entwurfszeichnung für den Schablonen-Wanddekor der Eingangshalle
Projet de décoration au pochoir pour le mur de l'entrée

Scotland Street School 1903–1906

Detail of the wrought-iron gate
Detail des schmiedeeisernen Tores
La grille en fer forgé, détail

Commissioned by the Govan School Board of Glasgow in 1903, Scotland Street School is undoubtedly the most modern of all Mackintosh's buildings and can be seen as an important harbinger of later Modern Movement architecture. Completed in October 1906, the school is dramatically utilitarian, with 21 classrooms designed to accommodate up to 1,250 children. Considerable financial constraints were placed on Mackintosh (the project's entire budget was only £15,000) and as a result there is only the barest of ornamentation. The twin stairwell towers provide the building with a verticality which contrasts with its otherwise strong horizontal emphasis. Where the use of glass in these towers was outstandingly modern, their conical roofs harked back to the staircase bays of traditional Scottish domestic architecture. The massive stairwells accommodated a large volume of foot traffic and the enormous windows ensured that the steps were well lit with natural light. These towers were a significant precursor to the enclosed glass and metal stairwells designed by Walter Gropius for his Model Factory and Office exhibited in Cologne in 1914—a building that belongs firmly to the Modern Movement. Although less noticeable, particularly from the ground, perhaps the most innovative elements of Scotland Street School are the two stepped banks of horizontal windows which flank each stairwell tower. This arrangement was to become a prominent feature of the Modern Movement and later post-war architecture.

Die 1903 vom Govan School Board, der örtlichen Schulbehörde, in Auftrag gegebene Scotland Street School ist zweifellos das modernste unter allen von Mackintosh entworfenen Bauwerken und kann als wichtiger Wegbereiter moderner Architektur gesehen werden. Das im Oktober 1906 vollendete Schulgebäude mit seinen 21 Klassenzimmern, die bis zu 1250 Schülern Platz boten, zeichnet sich durch seine Funktionalität aus. Der weitgehende Verzicht auf verzierendes Dekor resultierte jedoch nicht zuletzt aus den sehr knapp bemessenen finanziellen Mitteln (der Etat für das gesamte Bauprojekt betrug nur 15 000 Pfund). Durch die beiden Treppenhaustürme erhält die ansonsten vorherrschende Betonung der Horizontale ein starkes vertikales Gegengewicht. Die großflächige Verglasung der geräumigen Treppenhaustürme wirkt äußerst modern und sorgt für die notwendige Ausleuchtung mit Tageslicht. Dagegen verweisen die spitzen Kegeldächer der Türme auf traditionelle schottische Wohnhausarchitektur. Die Gestaltung der Treppenhaustürme scheint die 1914 von Walter Gropius für die Kölner Werkbundausstellung konzipierten, völlig verglasten Metall-Treppenhäuser für eine Musterfabrik und ein Bürogebäude vorwegzunehmen—Gebäude, die zu Synonymen der Moderne geworden sind. Die beiden übereinander versetzt angeordneten, waagerechten Fensterreihen, die die beiden Treppenhaustürme flankieren, bilden die vielleicht innovativsten Elemente der Scotland Street School und sollten zum auffallenden Merkmal der Moderne und später der Nachkriegsarchitektur werden.

Commandée par le Govan School Board, la Scotland Street School est sans doute le bâtiment le plus moderne jamais conçu par Mackintosh. On peut y voir une amorce de l'évolution ultérieure du Mouvement Moderne en architecture. Achevée en octobre 1906, elle répond à des con-traintes de programme drastiques: 21 classes pour 1 250 élèves, et un budget de 15 000 livres seulement. La décoration en est donc réduite au strict minimum. Les cages d'escalier jumelles inscrites dans des tours introduisent un élément de verticalité dans un bâtiment qui est par ailleurs strictement horizontal. Les vitrages des tours sont résolument modernes, mais les toits en poivrière relèvent de l'architecture écossaise traditionnelle. Les cages d'escalier sont gigantesques (Mackintosh a manifestement pensé aux centaines d'enfants qui allaient les emprunter). Elles sont éclairées par les immenses fenêtres des deux tours. Celles-ci annoncent l'escalier de verre et métal conçu par Walter Gropius pour son Usine et Bureaux modèles de l'Exposition de Cologne en 1914, bâtiment typique du Mouvement Moderne. Encore que moins visibles depuis la cour, les éléments les plus novateurs de l'école de Scotland Street sont les deux rangées de fenê-tres horizontales qui encadrent les cages d'escalier. Cette disposition devait être reprise par le Mouvement Moderne et l'architecture d'entre deux guerres.

RIGHT PAGE: The east stair tower
RECHTE SEITE: Der östliche Treppenturm
PAGE DE DROITE: La tour-escalier, côté est

SCHOOL BOARD ᴼ GLASGOW SCOTLAND STREET PVBLIC SCHOOL.

C R MACKINTOSH ARCHITECT
HONEYMAN KEPPIE & MACKINTOSH
140 BATH STREET GLASGOW

TOP: Perspective drawing, 1904
OBEN: Perspektivische Entwurfszeichnung
CI-DESSUS: Dessin en perspective

LEFT: General view from the north-east
LINKS: Gesamtansicht von Nordost
A GAUCHE: Vue générale du nord-est

LEFT PAGE: Window surround featuring carved stonework and inlaid tiles
LINKE SEITE: Fenstereinfassung mit Steinmetz-ornamenten und eingelegten Kacheln
PAGE DE GAUCHE: Encadrement de fenêtre en pierre sculptée et incrustations de faïence

TOP: School children lined up in formation in the assembly hall, c. 1920

OBEN: Die Aula mit Schulkindern in Reih und Glied

CI-DESSUS: Ecoliers en rangs dans le hall principal

RIGHT: The cookery demonstration room

RECHTS: Die Lehrküche

A DROITE: La salle de cours de cuisine

RIGHT PAGE: The stairwell

RECHTE SEITE: Das Treppenhaus

PAGE DE DROITE: La cage d'escalier

SCOTLAND STREET SCHOOL, GLASGOW, 1903–1906

Auchenibert
1904–1906

Detail of the roof with dormer window
Detail des Daches mit Gaube
Lucarne du toit

Situated on a hillside near Killearn, Auchenibert has an aura of a quiet nobility through its decorative restraint and use of dressed local stone. Having undoubtedly been severely constrained by his clients, the Shand family, to work within the Tudor style, Mackintosh designed the house in 1904 and building work was completed in 1906. Although Mackintosh visited Killearn frequently while Auchenibert was under construction, he too rarely climbed the steep hill to the house to see how the building work was proceeding, preferring instead to sit outside the village's public house. Needless to say, the Shands were not happy with this state of affairs and eventually another architect was hired to complete the project.

Durch den sparsamen Gebrauch dekorativer Details und die Verwendung behauener Natursteine erweckt das auf einem Hügel bei Killearn gelegene Landhaus Auchenibert den Eindruck vornehmer Zurückhaltung. Der Auftraggeber, die Familie Shand, hatte Mackintosh die Auflage gemacht, das Gebäude im Tudorstil zu errichten. Seine Entwürfe datieren aus dem Jahr 1904; die Bauarbeiten wurden 1906 beendet. Obwohl Mackintosh während der Bauarbeiten häufig nach Killearn reiste, bestieg er nur allzu selten den steilen Hügel, um sich vor Ort vom Fortgang der Bauarbeiten zu überzeugen. So überrascht es nicht, daß die Shands, unzufrieden mit dem Stand der Dinge, schließlich einen anderen Architekten mit der Fertigstellung ihres Hauses beauftragten.

Située sur une colline près de Killearn, la villa Auchenibert est d'une grande noblesse, grâce à sa taille, à la sobriété de sa décoration et à l'emploi de pierre locale appareillée. Mackintosh dessina les plans en 1904, et les travaux furent terminés en 1906. Il semble que les commanditaires, la famille Shand, aient insisté pour que le style soit «Tudor». Certes, Mackintosh a fait de fréquents séjours à Killearn au moment des travaux. Mais il prenait rarement la peine de grimper la colline pour surveiller le chantier et passait le plus clair de son temps à l'auberge du village. Naturellement, les Shand n'apprécièrent pas trop cette façon de travailler et finirent par engager un autre architecte.

General view
Gesamtansicht
Vue générale

Perspective drawing of the front façade
Perspektvische Entwurfszeichnung der Frontfassade
Dessin en perspective de la façade principale

INTERIORS FOR 6 FLORENTINE TERRACE 1906

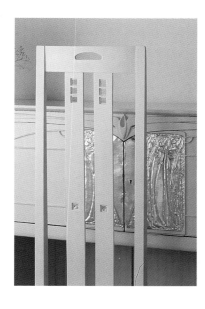

Detail of the drawing-room furnishings
Detail der Wohnzimmermöblierung
Mobilier du salon, détail

From 1906 to 1914, the Mackintoshes lived at 6 Florentine Terrace in the fashionable Hillhead area of Glasgow. The house was an unremarkable end-of-terrace Victorian property which the Mackintoshes substantially renovated inside. The interior was completely transformed by them into an outstanding series of jewel-like rooms which provided a suitably distinguished and highly aesthetic domestic setting. On the ground floor, the hallway and dining-room were rather sombre and gave no clue to the extraordinary lightness of the rooms above. The dining-room walls were covered in brown wrapping paper which was stencilled with a black trellis and pink rose motif. The fireplace was recycled from the Mackintoshes' Mains Street flat and was extended on either side with shelves.

Von 1906 bis 1914 wohnten die Mackintoshs in Hillhead, einem der vornehmsten Viertel Glasgows, in einem unscheinbaren viktorianischen Reihenhaus in der Florentine Terrace 6, das sie von Grund auf renovierten. Das Innere des Hauses verwandelten sie in eine Abfolge äußerst eleganter Räume, die ihrem häuslichen Leben einen höchst distinguierten und ästhetischen Rahmen gaben. Die Diele und das Speisezimmer im Erdgeschoß waren recht dunkel gehalten und hatten nichts mit der außerordentlichen Helligkeit der oberen Räume gemein. Die Wände des Speisezimmers waren mit braunem Packpapier tapeziert, auf das ein Schablonendekor aus schwarzem Gitterwerk und rosafarbenen Rosen aufgemalt war. Der Kamin im Speisezimmer, der von Bücherregalen flankiert wurde, stammte noch aus ihrer Wohnung in der Mains Street.

Les Mackintosh vécurent au 6 Florentine Terrace, dans le quartier chic de Hillhead, de 1906 à 1914. C'était une banale maison victorienne de fin de rangée, que les Mackintosh remanièrent complètement à l'intérieur. Cette remarquable série de pièces, de véritables bijoux, créait un cadre de vie distingué et éthéré, propre à impressionner les clients. Au rez-de-chaussée, l'entrée et la salle à manger étaient plutôt sombres et ne laissaient pas deviner l'extraordinaire luminosité de l'étage. Les murs de la salle à manger étaient tapissés de papier marron, décoré au pochoir d'un motif de treillage noir et de roses. La cheminée provenait de l'ancien appartement des Mackintosh à Mains Street, elle était encadrée de rayonnages supplémentaires.

The drawing-room
Das Wohnzimmer
Le salon

The entrance hall
Die Diele
Le hall d'entrée

The dining-room
Das Speisezimmer
La salle à manger

The studio
Das Atelier
L'atelier

In sharp contrast to the rooms below, the white drawing-room was an unworldly symphony of light and space. Sparsely furnished with furniture and fittings from the Mains Street flat, the drawing-room could be efficiently divided with curtains according to functional need. The floors were originally covered with white canvas but this was later replaced with a pale taupe carpet. The spirituality and purity of this most striking space is strongly evocative of Japanese interiors—an effect which would have been further heightened by the Mackintoshes' ikebana-style arrangements of foliage, flowers and twigs. In the white L-shaped master bedroom, the sculptural furniture, such as the spectacular cheval mirror, had been designed earlier in 1900 and came from the Mains Street flat. The fireplace and light-fittings, however, were created specifically for this room. The house was demolished in 1963 because of subsidence, but in 1981 it was reconstructed as part of the Hunterian Art Gallery about 100 metres away from the earlier site.

Einen scharfen Kontrast zu den Räumlichkeiten im unteren Geschoß bildete das weiße Wohnzimmer—eine überirdische Sinfonie aus Licht und Raum. Der nur spärlich mit Möbeln aus der Wohnung in der Mains Street ausgestattete Raum ließ sich, den jeweiligen Bedürfnissen entsprechend, durch Vorhänge teilen. Der Fußboden war ursprünglich mit weißem Segeltuch ausgelegt, das später durch einen hellen maulwurfsgrauen Teppich ersetzt wurde. Die Spiritualität und Reinheit dieses Raums erinnern an japanische Innenausstattungen—eine Wirkung, die durch die im Ikebana-Stil gebundenen Zweige und Blumen noch gesteigert wurde. Der Kamin und die Leuchten waren eigens für das L-förmige Schlafzimmer entworfen worden, während die Möbel, wie etwa der eindrucksvolle Standspiegel, bereits um 1900 entstanden waren und schon in der Mains Street benutzt worden waren. Eine Bodensenkung führte 1963 zum Abriß des Hauses; 1981 wurde es nur etwa 100 Meter entfernt als Teil der Hunterian Art Gallery rekonstruiert.

Contrastant avec les pièces du bas, le salon blanc évoquait une symphonie onirique de lumière et d'espace. Son mobilier se résumait à quelques meubles et objets apportés de l'appartement de Mains Street. Le salon pouvait être divisé selon les besoins par un rideau. Son parquet était à l'origine couvert d'une toile blanche, remplacée ensuite par une moquette gris pâle. La spiritualité et la pureté de cet espace étonnant évoquent les intérieurs japonais, effet encore accentué par les arrangements de fleurs, de feuilles et de branchages dans le style ikebana.Dans la chambre principale blanche en L, le mobilier imposant, qui comprenait un spectaculaire miroir en pied, avait été dessiné en 1900 et venait de l'appartement de Mains Street. Par contre, la cheminée et les lampes avaient été créées spécialement. La maison a été démolie en 1963, après un glissement de terrain. Elle a été reconstituée dans la Hunterian Art Gallery en 1981, à cent mètres environ du site d'origine.

INTERIORS FOR 6 FLORENTINE TERRACE (NOW 78 SOUTHPARK AVENUE), GLASGOW, 1906

The bedroom, fireplace wall
Das Schlafzimmer, Kaminseite
La chambre à coucher, côté cheminée

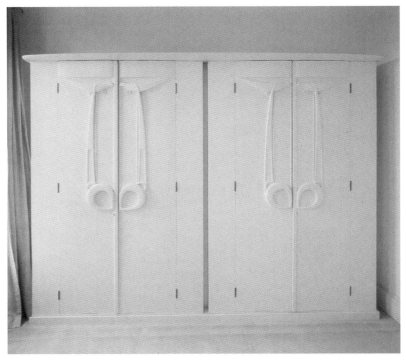

Wardrobes designed for the bedroom
Kleiderschränke, entworfen für das Schlafzimmer
Penderies conçues pour la chambre à coucher

Interiors and external Alterations for 78 Derngate 1916–1918 & 1919

Mrs. Bassett-Lowke at the rear of her house, 1916

Mrs. Bassett-Lowke vor der rückseitigen Fassade ihres Hauses

Mrs Bassett-Lowke devant la façade arrière de sa demeure

Unable to have a new house constructed due to wartime restrictions on new buildings, the industrialist Wynne J. Bassett-Lowke purchased 78 Derngate, a red-brick Victorian terraced house in Northampton, in 1915. Bassett-Lowke was a member of the Design and Industries Association and commissioned Mackintosh in early 1916 to remodel the interior and exterior of the house. The only detail altered on the front was a window, but to the rear of the property the kitchen and dining-room were extended, one above the other, while on the two upper floors two bedroom balconies were added. The rear elevation is a remarkable composition of geometric elements and can be considered the first example of Modern Movement architecture in Britain.

Da Neubauten während des Kriegs strengen Restriktionen unterlagen, erwarb der Industrielle Wynne J. Bassett-Lowke, ein Mitglied der Design and Industries Association, im Jahr 1915 Derngate 78, ein viktorianisches Reihenhaus aus rotem Backstein in Northampton. Anfang 1916 beauftragte er Mackintosh mit der Neugestaltung der Inneneinrichtung und der Fassaden. Während Mackintosh an der vorderen Fassade nur ein Fenster veränderte, erhielt die Rückseite des Gebäudes durch den Ausbau der Küche und des darüberliegenden Speisezimmers sowie den Anbau von zwei Schlafzimmerbalkonen in den beiden oberen Stockwerken einen völlig neuen Charakter. Diese Fassade mit ihrer bemerkenswerten Komposition aus geometrischen Formen kann als frühestes Beispiel modernistischer Architektur in Großbritannien angesehen werden.

Ne pouvant se faire construire une maison neuve en raison de l'interdiction de bâtir en temps de guerre, l'industriel Wynne J. Bassett-Lowke acheta en 1915 le numéro 78 Derngate, à Northampton. C'était une maison de briques en alignement, datant de l'époque victorienne. Bassett-Lowke faisait partie de la Design and Industries Association. Début 1916, il demanda à Mackintosh de rénover la maison. L'architecte ne modifia qu'une fenêtre en façade. Mais sur le jardin il agrandit la cuisine et la salle à manger au rez-de-chaussée et au premier étage. Il ajouta deux balcons pour les chambres aux étages supérieurs. La façade sur jardin est une remarquable composition géométrique qui s'inscrit déjà dans l'architecture du Mouvement Moderne en Grande-Bretagne.

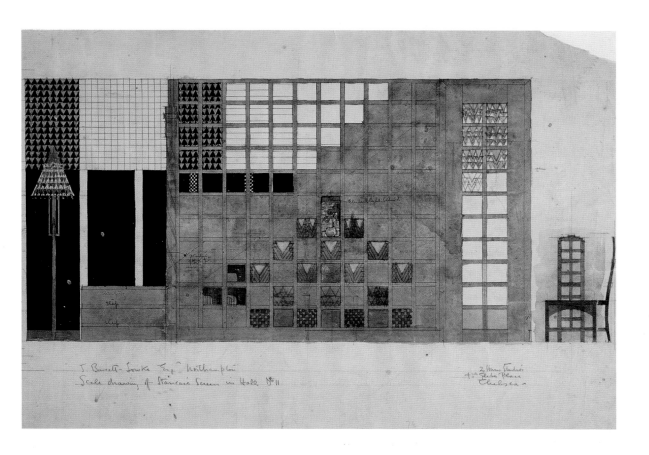

J. Bassett-Lowke Esq. Northampton
Scale drawing of Staircase Screen in Hall No. 11

2 Hans Studios
78 Glebe Place
Chelsea

TOP: Design for the staircase screen, 1916
OBEN: Entwurfszeichnung für die Verkleidung des Treppenaufganges
CI-DESSUS: Projet de lambrissage pour la cage d'escalier

LEFT: The entrance hall
LINKS: Die Diele
A GAUCHE: Le hall d'entrée

BOTTOM LEFT: The family gathered in the entrance hall
LINKS UNTEN: Familienversammlung in der Diele
CI-DESSOUS A GAUCHE: Photographie de famille dans le hall d'entrée

RIGHT: Chair designed for the guest room
RECHTS: Stuhl, entworfen für das Gästezimmer
A DROITE: Chaise conçue pour la chambre d'amis

RIGHT PAGE: The guest room
RECHTE SEITE: Das Gästezimmer
PAGE DE DROITE: La chambre d'amis

The interior scheme, incorporating bold geometric motifs, must have been rather intense. In the hall, the canary yellow, vermilion, emerald green, purple and lapis blue triangles set against a black background foreshadowed the Art Deco style. Bassett-Lowke, who was colour-blind, was thrilled with the interior and, in 1919, asked Mackintosh to redesign the guest bedroom. The resulting interior was perhaps Mackintosh's most radical—a theme of black and white stripes was set against rich accents of royal blue and emerald green. The geometric furniture designed for this room was inlaid with an early coloured plastic, indicating Mackintosh's interest in state-of-the-art materials. On showing his guest, George Bernard Shaw, to this bedroom, Bassett-Lowke is said to have remarked: "I trust the decor will not disturb your sleep", to which the Irish dramatist and critic replied: "No, I always sleep with my eyes closed."

Die Inneneinrichtung mit ihrer extravaganten geometrischen Formgebung muß eine enorme Ausstrahlung ausgeübt haben. In der Diele hoben sich kanariengelbe, zinnoberrote, smaragdgrüne, violette und lapislazuliblaue Dreiecke lebhaft von einem schwarzen Hintergrund ab— eine Vorwegnahme des Art-déco-Stils. Der farbenblinde Bassett-Lowke war begeistert und bat Mackintosh 1919 auch das Gästezimmer neu zu gestalten. Das Ergebnis war Mackintoshs vielleicht radikalste Inneneinrichtung: Dominierendes Element war ein schwarzweißes Streifenmuster, das sich scharf von königsblauen und smaragdgrünen Farbakzenten absetzte. Das geometrische Mobiliar war mit einem gerade neuerfundenen farbigen Kunststoff intarsiert, was Mackintoshs Interesse an zeitgemäßen Werkstoffen belegt. Als Bassett-Lowke seinen Gast George Bernard Shaw in dieses Schlafzimmer geleitete, soll er zu ihm gesagt haben: „Ich hoffe, daß Sie sich durch das Dekor nicht in Ihrem Schlaf gestört fühlen." Die Antwort des irischen Dramatikers und Kritikers: „Aber nein, ich schlafe stets mit geschlossenen Augen."

L'intérieur, avec ses motifs géométriques audacieux, devait être légèrement angoissant. Dans l'entrée, des séries de triangles jaune canari, vermillon, vert émeraude, violet et bleu lapis-lazuli se détachaient sur un fond sombre. Ces motifs évoquent déjà le style Art déco. Bassett-Lowke—qui était du reste daltonien—fut enchanté de ce décor. Il demanda donc à Mackintosh en 1919 de refaire la chambre d'amis. Le résultat est sans conteste le plus révolutionnaire de la carrière de Mackintosh: des zébrures noir et blanc sur un fond bleu roi et vert émeraude. Le mobilier géométrique conçu pour cette pièce était incrusté de matière plastique colorée (matériau qui venait d'être découvert), ce qui montre bien l'intérêt porté par Mackintosh aux matériaux les plus récents. On raconte qu'en montrant sa chambre à George Bernard Shaw, Bassett-Lowke lui aurait déclaré: «J'espère que le décor ne vous empêchera point de dormir.» Ce à quoi Shaw rétorqua: «Mais non, je dors toujours les yeux fermés.»

Project for Studio Houses 1920

On 8 January 1920, the painter Harold Squire asked Mackintosh to design a studio house for him in Glebe Place, Chelsea. A few weeks later, Mackintosh was approached by the sculptor, F. Derwent Wood, and the designer, A. Blunt, to design similar neighbouring schemes for themselves. Unfortunately, for reasons probably due to cost or lack of planning consent, these two additional studio houses were never realized. The initial scheme for Squire's studio house involved a three-storey building with a roof garden. This was deemed far too costly, however, and Squire asked Mackintosh to revise the plans so that costs would not exceed £6,000. The final design incorporated two buildings: a house and a studio to the rear. While Squire was apparently pleased with the project on its completion, he only spent two years in the building, as it was too expensive for him to maintain. Although Harold Squire's studio house is extant, it has been extensively altered.

Am 8. Januar 1920 beauftragte der Maler Harold Squire Mackintosh mit dem Bau eines Atelierhauses am Glebe Place in Chelsea. Wenige Wochen später traten der Bildhauer F. Derwent Wood und der Designer A. Blunt an Mackintosh mit der Bitte heran, auch für sie in unmittelbarer Nachbarschaft von Squires Atelierhaus ähnliche Häuser zu entwerfen. Die beiden letzteren Projekte wurden allerdings—sei es aus Kostengründen oder wegen planerischer Mängel—nie realisiert. Der ursprüngliche Entwurf für Squires Atelierhaus, der einen dreigeschossigen Bau mit Dachgarten vorsah, wurde von seinem Auftraggeber als zu kostspielig verworfen. Squire bat Mackintosh um eine Überarbeitung der Pläne, weil der Bauetat von 6 000 Pfund nicht überschritten werden sollte. Der endgültige Entwurf umfaßte schließlich zwei Gebäudeteile, ein Wohnhaus und ein dahinter liegendes Atelier. Obgleich Squire offenbar mit dem Ergebnis zufrieden war, lebte er nur zwei Jahre in dem neuen Haus, da es sich im Unterhalt als zu kostspielig erwies. Das Atelierhaus von Harold Squire ist noch erhalten, unterlag jedoch inzwischen beträchtlichen baulichen Veränderungen.

Le 8 janvier 1920, le peintre Harold Squire demanda à Mackintosh de lui dessiner une maison-atelier à Glebe Place, Chelsea. Quelques semaines plus tard, le sculpteur F. Derwent Wood et le décorateur A. Blunt commandèrent des projets identiques pour le même quartier. Sans doute par manque de fonds, ou faute d'avoir obtenu le permis de construire, ces deux ateliers supplémentaires ne furent jamais réalisés. Le projet initial pour l'atelier de Squire se développait sur trois niveaux, avec toit-terrasse. Squire demanda à Mackintosh de revoir ses plans afin que le coût de construction ne dépasse pas les 6 000 livres sterling. Le projet final réunissait deux bâtiments: la maison et l'atelier à l'arrière. Apparemment satisfait du projet terminé, Squire n'y passa pourtant que deux ans, les frais d'entretien étant trop élevés. La maison existe toujours, mais elle a été radicalement transformée.

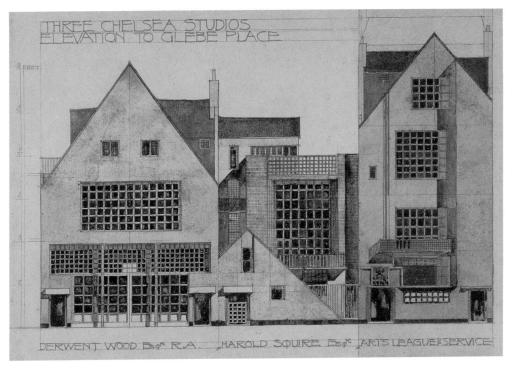

Elevation of the front façades of the studio house for Harold Squire and neighbouring buildings, 1920

Aufriß der Frontfassaden für das Atelierhaus von Harold Squire und die angrenzenden Gebäude

Elévation de la façade principale de la maison-atelier de Harold Squire et des immeubles environnants

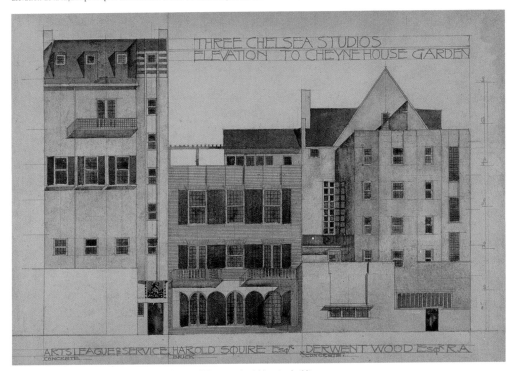

Elevation of the rear façades of the studio house for Harold Squire and neighbouring buildings, 1920

Aufriß der rückseitigen Fassaden des Atelierhauses von Harold Squire und der angrenzenden Gebäude

Elévation de la façade arrière de la maison-atelier de Harold Squire et des immeubles environnants

PROJECT FOR A BLOCK OF STUDIO FLATS FOR THE ARTS LEAGUE OF SERVICE 1920

Members of the Arts League of Service, a group that the Mackintoshes were closely involved with, conceived an ambitious plan to develop a large block of studio flats in Chelsea. Around this time, artists were finding it extremely difficult to locate suitable studio space, because many of the previously existing studios had been converted into living accommodation during the war. The idea was that the Arts League of Service would finance the project on a co-operative basis, with each artist being a shareholder as well as a tenant. A site adjacent to Harold Squire's studio was chosen for the project and on 31 March 1920, Mackintosh was requested to draw up plans for the building. After being accepted by the League, the design was submitted for planning approval and was almost immediately criticized for being too factory-like in appearance, with insufficient decorative elements of the façade. In one heated meeting between Mackintosh and the Church Commissioners' architect, the latter, referring to the proposed scheme, declared: "My dear Sir! This isn't architecture!" and began amending the drawings with all manner of classical detail. Mackintosh, intransigent as ever, swore that he would give up architecture altogether if his plans were not approved. Some weeks later, the project did receive planning approval but was abandoned, probably due to lack of funding.

Die Mitglieder der Arts League of Service—einer Vereinigung zur Förderung der Künste, der die Mackintoshs eng verbunden waren—hatten den ehrgeizigen Plan entwickelt, in Chelsea ein großes Appartementhaus mit integrierten Ateliers zu errichten. Für Künstler war es damals äußerst schwierig, geeignete Atelierräume zu finden, da während des Krieges viele der vorhandenen Ateliers zu Wohnungen umgewandelt worden waren. Das Bauprojekt sollte auf Genossenschaftsbasis finanziert werden: Jeder Künstler sollte sowohl Anteilseigner als auch Mieter sein. Für das geplante Gebäude wurde ein Grundstück ausgewählt, das an das Atelier von Harold Squire angrenzte, und am 31. März 1920 erhielt Mackintosh den offiziellen Auftrag, Entwürfe für dieses Projekt zu liefern. Die Arts League of Service akzeptierte Mackintoshs Entwürfe, aber die zuständige Baubehörde verweigerte zunächst die Genehmigung und kritisierte, daß das Gebäude wie eine Fabrik aussehe und zu wenig Fassadenschmuck aufweise. In einer erregten Auseinandersetzung zwischen Mackintosh und dem Architekten der zuständigen Kirchenkommission, rief dieser aus: „Mein lieber Mann! Das ist keine Architektur!", ehe er begann, die Entwürfe im Sinne seiner klassischen Kunstauffassung zu „verbessern". Mackintosh, unnachgiebig wie immer, schwor, daß er nie wieder als Architekt arbeiten werde, wenn seine Pläne nicht genehmigt würden. Einige Wochen später wurde die Bauerlaubnis schließlich doch erteilt, das Projekt jedoch später, wahrscheinlich aus Geldmangel, aufgegeben.

Le couple Mackintosh était très proche de la Arts League of Service, coopérative d'artistes, qui envisageait de construire un immeuble de studios à Chelsea. Les ateliers d'artistes étaient alors très difficiles à trouver, car ils avaient été transformés en logements pendant la guerre. Le concept retenu était le suivant: la Arts League financerait le projet, et tous les artistes seraient actionnaires en même temps que locataires. Une parcelle proche de l'atelier de Harold Squire et appartenant à l'Eglise anglicane fut retenue, et le 31 mars 1920 Mackintosh fut appelé à dessiner les plans. Accepté par la League, le projet fut soumis à la procédure d'obtention du permis de construire. Il fut alors très violemment critiqué: on lui reprochait notamment de ressembler à une usine et la façade de manquer d'éléments décoratifs. Lors d'une discussion houleuse qui l'opposait à Mackintosh, l'architecte en chef de l'Eglise anglicane finit par s'exclamer: «Mais cher monsieur, ce n'est pas de l'architecture!» Et il se mit à corriger le projet de Mackintosh en y ajoutant force détails classiques. Plus têtu que jamais, Mackintosh jura qu'il abandonnerait l'architecture si ses plans n'étaient pas approuvés. Le permis de construire fut finalement accordé quelques semaines plus tard, mais le projet fut abandonné faute de financement.

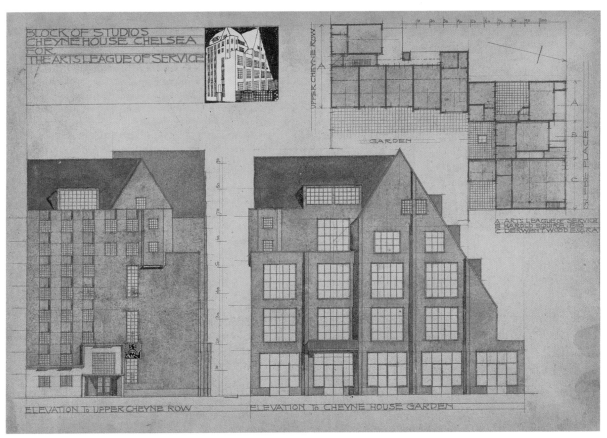

Perspective drawing of the façade, ground plan and elevations of studios planned for the Arts League of Service, 1920

Perspektivischer Fassadenentwurf, Grundriß und Aufrisse für das geplante Ateliergebäude der Arts League of Service

Dessin en perspective de la façade, coupe horizontale et élévations de façades d'ateliers, plans pour la Arts League of Service

Carnations and Stripes, 1915–23
Nelken und Streifen
Œillets et rayures
18 x 32 cm

Stylized Dahlias, 1915–23
Stilisierte Dahlien
Dahlias stylisés
20.3 x 12.5 cm

Bouquet, 1915–23
Blumenstrauß
Bouquet
41.4 x 33.7 cm

Rose and Teardrop, 1915–23
Rose und Träne
Rose et larme
25.5 x 25.5 cm

RIGHT PAGE | RECHTE SEITE | PAGE DE DROITE:
Odalisque, 1915–23
Odaliske
Odalisque
20.2 x 12.7 cm

Stylized Flowers and Checkerwork, 1915–23
Stilisierte Blumen und Schachbrettmuster
Fleurs stylisées et damier
24 x 20.3 cm

Stylized Petals with Teardrops, 1915–23
Stilisierte Blütenblätter mit Tränen
Pétales stylisés et larmes
32.5 x 28.3 cm

Orange and Purple Spirals, 1915–23
Orange und purpurne Spiralen
Spirales oranges et violettes
10.8 x 14.1 cm

Waves, 1915–23
Wellen
Vagues
26.5 x 22 cm

A partir de 1900, Mackintosh a moins de temps pour peindre et se consacre surtout à des études de fleurs. En 1901, pendant ses vacances à Holy Island (Lindisfarne), il applique pour la première fois des lavis diaphanes sur ses dessins au crayon. Il réalisera beaucoup d'études de fleurs dans les années qui suivent. Avant 1915, c'est surtout la flore sauvage qui l'intéresse. La couleur des lavis devient plus saturée et le trait plus stylisé. Dans ses carnets, les aquarelles d'une grande précision botanique—et qui révèlent une main plus sûre que dans les œuvres symbolistes antérieures—côtoient les croquis de bâtiments. Elles sont souvent signées «M.T.» (Margaret et Toshie) ou «MMM CRM» (ce qui semblerait indiquer la présence, mais non la collaboration, de Margaret).

Pendant son séjour à Walberswick, au Suffolk, entre 1914 et 1915, Mackintosh réalise une trentaine d'études de fleurs dont certaines sont destinées à un portfolio qui doit être édité en Allemagne. La déclaration de guerre vient interrompre le projet. Les études de 1914 sont plus décoratives et accomplies que les précédentes. Elles sont aussi plus spontanées que celles de 1915, manifestement réalisées dans un format standard convenant à la publication.

Lorsqu'il s'installe à Londres en 1915, Mackintosh essaie de gagner sa vie avec sa peinture. Le choix de fleurs cultivées et non plus sauvages, par exemple les *Anemones* (Anémones, ill. p. 161) de 1916 est sans doute une concession au goût du plus grand nombre. Les dernières œuvres de cette période, par exemple *The Grey Iris* de 1922-24 sont plus stylisées et abstraites; les couleurs se font plus vives et plus nettes. L'artiste semble captivé par le jeu de la lumière sur les différentes surfaces. Cette fascination ne fera que s'accentuer par la suite.

Pendant son séjour en France, de 1923 à 1927, Mackintosh ne peint pratiquement que des paysages: bâtiments isolés, petits villages, coins de rue. La juxtaposition de plans de couleur, caractéristique des œuvres de cette période, révèle l'influence des post-impressionnistes, notamment de Paul Cézanne (1839–1906). Le scintillement de la lumière et la vigueur des masses sont très perceptibles dans *La Ville*, Port-Vendres (ill. p. 161) et *Le Fort Maillert* (ill. p. 167), entre autres. Il se dégage de ces paysages—où l'on reconnaît sans peine l'œil de l'architecte sensible à l'articulation des volumes—une force que l'on trouve rarement dans des aquarelles.

«L'art est la fleur—L'art est la feuille verte. Laissons chaque artiste faire de sa fleur un bel objet vivant (...) Vous devez offrir les fleurs de l'art qui est en vous— les symboles de tout ce qui est noblesse, beauté et source d'inspiration.» (Charles Rennie Mackintosh, *Seemliness-lecture*, 1902).

Anemones, c. 1916
Anemonen
Anémones
50.5 x 49.5 cm

La Ville, Port-Vendres, c. 1924-26
46 x 46 cm

Cabbages in an Orchard, 1894
Kohlköpfe im Obstgarten | Choux dans un verger
8.6 x 23.6 cm

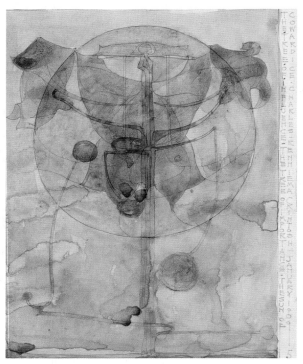

The Tree of Influence, 1895
Der Baum des Einflusses
L'Arbre de l'Influence
21.4 x 17.2 cm

The Tree of Personal Effort, 1895
Der Baum der persönlichen Bemühung
L'Arbre de l'Effort Personnel
21.1 x 17.4 cm

The Harvest Moon, 1892
Der Herbstmond | La Lune de la Moisson
35.2 x 27.6 cm

Sea Pink, Holy Island, 1901

Strand-Lichtnelke | Œillet de Mer

25.8 x 20.2 cm

Elder, Walberswick, 1915

Holunder | Sureau

26.2 x 20.6 cm

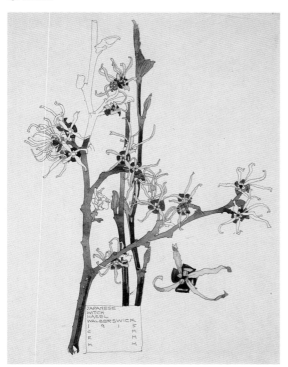

Japanese Witch Hazel, Walberswick, 1915

Japanischer Zauberstrauch | Coudrier japonais

26.3 x 21.1 cm

Willow-herb, Buxstead, 1919

Weidenröschen | Liane de saule

25.8 x 20 cm

Fritillaria, Walberswick, 1915
Kaiserkrone | Fritillaire
25.3 x 20.2 cm

La Rue de Soleil, Port-Vendres, 1926
40.5 x 39 cm

The Little Bay, Port-Vendres, 1927
Die kleine Bucht | La Petite Baie
39.3 x 39.4 cm

Le Fort Maillert, 1927
35.8 x 28.5 cm

CHRONOLOGY

1868 Charles Rennie Mackintosh is born on 7 June in Glasgow.

1875 Attends Reid's Public School, Glasgow.

1877 Attends Alan Glen's High School, Glasgow.

1884 Begins professional apprenticeship at the architectural practice of John Hutchison, Glasgow, and enrols in painting and drawing evening classes at the Glasgow School of Art.

1885 Francis H. Newbery is appointed director of the Glasgow School of Art.

1889 Joins the newly established architectural practice of Honeyman & Keppie, Glasgow.

1890 Awarded the Alexander Thomson Scholarship for his design for "A Public Hall".
Awarded a National Silver Medal at South Kensington for his design for "A Science and Art Museum".
His first building commission: Redclyffe, a pair of semidetached houses in Glasgow for his uncle, William Hamilton.

1891 Scholarship tour to Italy, returning via Paris, Brussels, Antwerp and London.
Delivers *Scottish Baronial Architecture* paper to the Glasgow Architectural Association.
The sisters Frances and Margaret Macdonald enrol as painting day students at the Glasgow School of Art.

1892 Enters Soane Medallion Competition with his design for "A Chapter House" which is subsequently awarded the National Gold Medal at South Kensington.

1893 Delivers *Architecture* paper to the Glasgow Institute.
Starts on designs for the Glasgow Herald building (completed in 1895).

1894 Begins designs for Queen Margaret's Medical College (completed in 1896).
First joint exhibition with his friend Herbert MacNair and the Macdonald sisters—later the Glasgow Four.

1895 Commences design for Martyrs' Public School (completed in 1896).

1896 Begins proposal for the Glasgow School of Art Competition.
Stencil decorations for the Buchanan Street Tea Rooms.
Exhibits with The Four at the Arts & Crafts Society Exhibition, London.

1897 Building of the Glasgow School of Art commences (first stage completed in 1899).
Designs St. Matthew's Free Church (later to become Queen's Cross Church).
Designs furniture for the Argyle Street Tea Rooms.

1898 Designs an Industrial Hall for the Glasgow International Exhibition of 1901.
Receives first foreign commission—a dining-room for H. Bruckmann, Munich.

1899 The new Glasgow School of Art opens.
Designs Windyhill for the Davidson family (completed in 1901 with additions in 1905).
Frances Macdonald and Herbert MacNair marry and move to Liverpool.
Begins interior design of his flat at 120 Mains Street (completed in 1900).

1900 Marries Margaret Macdonald at St. Augustine's Church, Dumbarton.
Designs furniture and interior decorations for the Ingram Street Tea Rooms (with further additions in 1902).
Exhibits with The Four at the Eighth Secessionist Exhibition, Vienna.

1901 Designs Daily Record building, Glasgow.
Enters "Haus eines Kunstfreundes" (House for an Art Lover) competition; awarded special prize.
Commissioned by Mrs. Rowat to design interior of 14 Kingsborough Gardens (completed in 1902).
Designs the Gate Lodge, Auchenbothie, Kilmacolm.

1902 Exhibits at the International Exhibition of Modern Decorative Art, Turin.
Commissioned by Fritz Wärndorfer to design a music salon, Vienna.
Commissioned by Walter Blackie to design Hill House (completed in 1905).
Prepares plans for the Liverpool Anglican Cathedral competition.
Delivers *Seemliness* paper, most probably to the Northern Art Worker's Guild, Manchester.

1903 Exhibits in Moscow.
Designs the Willow Tea Rooms (completed and opened in 1904).
Exhibits a bedroom at the "Dresdener Werkstätten für Handwerkskunst" Exhibition, Dresden.

1904 Mackintosh is made a partner in the firm of Honeyman & Keppie.
Designs Scotland Street School for the Govan School Board (completed in 1906).
Commissioned by Mrs. Catherine Cranston and her husband, Major John Cochrane, to design the interior of their home, Hous'hill (mainly completed in 1905 with additions in 1909).
Commissioned by F. J. Shand to design Auchenibert, near Killearn (completed 1906).

1905 Commissioned by A. S. Ball to design a dining-room, Berlin.

1906 Designs new boardroom for the Glasgow School of Art.
Redesigns the second phase of building work for the School of Art (finishes designs in 1907).
The Mackintoshes move to 6 Florentine Terrace.
Designs the "Dutch Kitchen" for the Argyle Street Tea Rooms.

Commissioned by H. B.Collins to design Mosside, (later Cloak), Kilmacolm (with alterations undertaken in 1912).
Elected a Fellow of the Royal Institute of British Architects.

1907 Designs the Oak Room for the Ingram Street Tea Rooms.

1909 Second phase of building work at the Glasgow School of Art completed.
Exhibits at the Kunstschau, Vienna.

1911 Designs the Cloister Room and the Chinese Room for the Ingram Street Tea Rooms.

1913 Mackintosh leaves Honeyman & Keppie.

1914 The Mackintoshes spend most of the year in Walberswick, Suffolk, and produce a series of flower studies.

1915 The Mackintoshes move to London.

1916 Designs ranges of textiles for Foxton's and Sefton's, both in London.
Commissioned by W. J. Bassett-Lowke to remodel the exterior and interior of 78 Derngate, Northampton (completed in 1917).

1917 Designs "The Dug-Out" for the Willow Tea Rooms.

1920 Designs three Chelsea studios (only one is built for Harold Squire).
Designs a block of studios for the Arts League of Service in Chelsea (unexecuted).
Designs a theatre for Margaret Morris in Chelsea (unexecuted).

1923 The Mackintoshes move to Port-Vendres, France.
Exhibits watercolours at the Fifth International Exhibition, Chicago, and in London.

1927 Returns to London.
Undergoes medical treatment for cancer of the tongue.

1928 Charles Rennie Mackintosh dies in London on 10 December.

1933 Margaret Macdonald dies in London.
Memorial exhibition of Mackintosh's work held in Glasgow.

CHRONOLOGIE

1868   Charles Rennie Mackintosh wird am 7. Juni in Glasgow geboren.

1875   Wird Schüler der Reid's Public School, Glasgow.

1877   Wird Schüler der Alan Glen's High School, Glasgow.

1884   Beginn einer Ausbildung im Architekturbüro von John Hutchison, Glasgow; er schreibt sich für Abendkurse an der Glasgow School of Art ein.

1885   Francis H. Newbery wird zum Direktor der Glasgow School of Art ernannt.

1889   Anstellung im neu gegründeten Architekturbüro von John Honeyman & Keppie, Glasgow.

1890   Gewinnt das Alexander-Thomson-Reisestipendium für seinen Entwurf einer „Public Hall".
Auszeichnung mit einer Silbermedaille vom South Kensington Museum für den Entwurf eines „Science and Art Museum".
Erhält von seinem Onkel, William Hamilton, seinen ersten Bauauftrag: Redclyffe, ein Doppelhaus in Glasgow.

1891   Studienreise nach Italien; Rückkehr via Paris, Brüssel, Antwerpen und London.
Vor der Glasgow Architectural Association hält er einen Vortrag mit dem Titel *Scottish Baronial Architecture* (schottische Feudalarchitektur).
Die Schwestern Frances und Margaret Macdonald schreiben sich als ordentliche Studentinnen der Malerei an der Glasgow School of Art ein.

1892   Reicht beim Soane Medallion Wettbewerb den Entwurf „Chapter House" (Kapitelsaal) ein, der daraufhin vom South Kensington Museum mit einer Goldmedaille ausgezeichnet wird.

1893   Vor dem Glasgow Institute hält er einen Vortrag mit dem Titel *Architecture*.
Erste Entwürfe für das Bürogebäude des Glasgow Herald (1895 fertiggestellt).

1894   Entwürfe für das Queen Margaret's Medical College (1896 fertiggestellt).
Erste gemeinsame Ausstellung mit seinem Freund Herbert MacNair und den Macdonald-Schwestern—den späteren „Glasgow Four" (Glasgow Vier).

1895   Entwürfe für die Martyrs' Public School (1896 fertiggestellt).

1896   Beitrag zum Wettbewerb der Glasgow School of Art.
Schablonen-Wanddekore für die Buchanan Street Tea Rooms.
Die Glasgow Four nehmen an der Ausstellung der Arts-and-Crafts-Society in London teil.

1897   Baubeginn der Glasgow School of Art (Fertigstellung des ersten Bauabschnitts 1899).
Entwürfe für die St. Matthew's Free Church (die spätere Queen's Cross Church).
Möbelentwürfe für die Argyle Street Tea Rooms.

1898 Entwurf einer „Industrial Hall" (Ausstellungshalle für Industriegüter) für die Internationale Ausstellung in Glasgow 1901.
Erhält den ersten Auftrag aus dem Ausland: ein Speisezimmer für H. Bruckmann, München.

1899 Eröffnung der neuen Glasgow School of Art.
Entwurf des Landhauses Windyhill für die Familie Davidson (1901 fertiggestellt, 1905 erweitert).
Frances Macdonald und Herbert MacNair heiraten und ziehen nach Liverpool.
Beginnt mit den Entwürfen für die Inneneinrichtung seiner Wohnung in der Mains Street 120 (1900 fertiggestellt).

1900 Heirat mit Margaret Macdonald in der St. Augustine's Church in Dumbarton.
Entwurf der Inneneinrichtung für die Ingram Street Tea Rooms (1902 weitere Ergänzungen).
Beteiligung an der Achten Ausstellung der Wiener Sezession.

1901 Entwurf eines Büro- und Geschäftshauses für den Daily Record.
Beteiligung an dem Wettbewerb für das „Haus eines Kunstfreundes". Sein Beitrag wird mit einem Sonderpreis ausgezeichnet.
Wird von Mrs. Rowat beauftragt, die Innenausstattung von Kingsborough Gardens 14 zu entwerfen (1902 fertiggestellt).
Entwirft das Gate Lodge in Auchenbothie, Kilmacolm.

1902 Beteiligung an der Internationalen Ausstellung für moderne dekorative Kunst in Turin.
Wird von Fritz Wärndorfer beauftragt, einen Musiksalon zu entwerfen.
Für den Verleger Walter Blackie entwirft er das Landhaus Hill House (1905 fertiggestellt).
Erste Entwürfe für den Wettbewerb der Liverpool Anglican Cathedral.
Hält—wahrscheinlich vor der Northern Art Workers' Guild in Manchester—seine *Seemliness-Lecture* (Vorlesung über Schicklichkeit).

1903 Ausstellungsbeteiligung in Moskau.
Entwürfe für die Inneneinrichtung der Willow Tea Rooms (1904 fertiggestellt und eröffnet).
Nimmt mit einem Schlafzimmerentwurf an der Ausstellung der Dresdener Werkstätten für Handwerkskunst in Dresden teil.

1904 Mackintosh wird Teilhaber des Architekturbüros Honeyman & Keppie.
Im Auftrag des Govan School Board, der örtlichen Schulbehörde, entwirft er die Scotland Street School (1906 fertiggestellt).
Für Catherine Cranston und ihren Gatten Major John Cochrane entwirft er die Innenausstattung ihres Hauses Hous'hill (1905 weitgehend fertiggestellt, 1909 erweitert).
Für F. J. Shand entwirft er das Landhaus Auchenibert bei Killearn (1906 fertiggestellt).

1905 Entwurf eines Speisezimmers für A. S. Ball, Berlin.

1906 Entwurf eines neuen Konferenzsaales für die Glasgow School of Art.
Revidiert die Entwürfe für den zweiten Bauabschnitt der Glasgow School of Art (1907 abgeschlossen).
Umzug der Mackintoshs in die Florentine Terrace 6.
Entwurf der „Dutch Kitchen" (Holländischen Küche) für die Argyle Street Tea Rooms.
Im Auftrag von H. B. Collins entwirft er Mosside (später Cloak) in Kilmacolm (bauliche Änderungen 1912).
Wird zum Mitglied des Royal Institute of British Architects gewählt.

1907 Entwurf des „Oak Room" (Eichenzimmer) für die Ingram Street Tea Rooms.

1909 Ende des zweiten Bauabschnitts der Glasgow School of Art.
Ausstellungsbeteiligung an der Kunstschau Wien.

1911 Entwurf des „Cloister Room" (Klosterraum) und des „Chinese Room" (Chinesisches Zimmer) für die Ingram Street Tea Rooms.

1913 Mackintosh verläßt das Architekturbüro Honeyman & Keppie.

1914 Aufenthalt in Walberswick, Suffolk. Beschäftigung mit Pflanzenaquarellen.

1915 Umzug der Mackintoshs nach London.

1916 Wird von den Firmen Foxton's und Sefton's mit dem Entwurf von Textildesigns beauftragt.
W. J. Bassett-Lowke beauftragt ihn mit der Neugestaltung der Fassade und der Inneneinrichtung des Hauses Derngate 78 in Northampton (1917 fertiggestellt).

1917 Entwurf des „Dug-Out"-Raums für die Willow Tea Rooms.

1920 Entwurf von drei Atelierhäusern in Chelsea (nur das Haus für Harold Squire wird realisiert).
Entwurf eines Wohnblocks mit integrierten Ateliers für die Arts League of Service in Chelsea (nicht realisiert).
Entwurf eines Theaters für Margaret Morris (nicht realisiert).

1923 Die Mackintoshs lassen sich in Port-Vendres, Frankreich, nieder.
Seine Aquarelle werden in Chicago auf der 5. Internationalen Ausstellung und in London ausgestellt.

1927 Rückkehr nach London.
Mackintosh erkrankt an Zungenkrebs.

1928 Am 10. Dezember stirbt Charles Rennie Mackintosh.

1933 Margaret Macdonald stirbt in London.
In Glasgow findet eine Mackintosh-Gedächtnisausstellung statt.

CHRONOLOGIE

1868 Charles Rennie Mackintosh naît le 7 juin à Glasgow.

1875 Fréquente la Reid's Public School de Glasgow.

1877 Fréquente la Alan Glen's High School, Glasgow.

1884 Entre en apprentissage à l'agence d'architecture de John Hutchison à Glasgow et suit des cours du soir (peinture et dessin) à la Glasgow School of Art.

1885 Francis H. Newbery est nommé directeur de la Glasgow School of Art.

1889 Entre dans la nouvelle agence d'architecture Honeyman & Keppie à Glasgow.

1890 Obtient la bourse d'études Alexander Thompson pour son projet «A Public Hall».
Remporte la médaille nationale d'argent à South Kensington pour son projet «A Science and Art Museum» (musée des sciences et des arts).
Son oncle William Hamilton lui passe sa première commande de bâtiment: Redclyffe.

1891 Voyage d'études en Italie. Au retour, passe par Paris, Bruxelles, Anvers et Londres.
Donne une conférence sur la *Scottish Baronial Architecture* (l'Architecture féodale écossaise) pour la Glasgow Architectural Association.
Les sœurs Frances et Margaret Macdonald suivent pendant la journée les cours de peinture de la Glasgow School of Art.

1892 Participation au concours Soane Medallion avec son projet pour «Chapter House» qui remportera la médaille d'or nationale à South Kensington.

1893 Conférence sur *L'Architecture* devant le Glasgow Institute.
Commence le projet du bâtiment du Glasgow Herald (achevé en 1895).

1894 Commence les plans du Queen Margaret's Medical College (achevé en 1896).
Première exposition avec son ami Herbert MacNair et les sœurs Macdonald—ils formeront le groupe appelé plus tard «The Glasgow Four» (Les Quatre de Glasgow).

1895 Plans de la Martyrs' Public School (achevée en 1896).

1896 Commence un projet pour le concours de la Glasgow School of Art.
Décorations au pochoir pour le Buchanan Street Tea Rooms.
Les Quatre de Glasgow participent à l'exposition londonienne de la Arts & Crafts Society.

1897 Commencement des travaux de la Glasgow School of Art (première phase terminée en 1899).
Projet pour St. Matthew's Free Church (rebaptisée plus tard Queen's Cross).
Dessine les meubles du Argyle Street Tea Rooms.

1898 Dessine un «Industrial Hall» (Palais de l'Industrie) pour l'Exposition internationale de Glasgow de 1901.
Reçoit sa première commande de l'étranger, une salle à manger pour H. Bruckmann à Munich.

1899 La nouvelle Glasgow School of Art ouvre ses portes.
Dessine la villa Windyhill pour la famille Davidson (achevée en 1901 et agrandie en 1905).
Mariage de Frances Macdonald et de Herbert MacNair. Les époux s'installent à Liverpool.
Mackintosh entreprend la décoration intérieure de son appartement du 120 Mains Street (achevée en 1900).

1900 Epouse Margaret Macdonald en l'église St. Augustine de Dumbarton.
Dessine le mobilier et la décoration intérieure du Ingram Street Tea Rooms (des modifications seront apportées en 1902).
Participe à la Huitième Exposition de la Sécession à Vienne.

1901 Projet pour l'immeuble du Daily Record à Glasgow.
Participe au concours «Haus eines Kunstfreundes» (Maison pour un amateur d'art) et remporte un prix spécial.
Intérieurs de la maison du 14 Kingsborough Gardens pour Mrs Rowat (projet achevé en 1902).
Dessine la Gate Lodge à Auchenbothie, Kilmacolm.

1902 Participe à l'Exposition internationale d'art décoratif moderne à Turin.
Salon de musique pour Fritz Wärndorfer à Vienne.
Conçoit la villa Hill House pour Walter Blackie (achevée en 1905).
Prépare des plans pour le concours de la Liverpool Anglican Cathedral.
Donne une conférence intitulée Seemliness (l'Harmonie), très probablement devant la Northern Art Worker's Guild à Manchester.

1903 Exposition à Moscou.
Décore le Willow Tea Rooms (achevé et inauguré en 1904).
Présente une chambre à coucher à l'exposition «Dresdener Werkstätten für Handwerkskunst» de Dresde.

1904 Mackintosh devient associé de l'agence Honeyman & Keppie.
Dessine la Scotland Street School pour le Govan School Board (achevée en 1906).
Catherine Cranston et son époux, le Major John Cochrane, lui commandent la décoration intérieure de leur maison, Hous'hill (achevée en grande partie en 1905 et agrandie en 1909).
Conçoit la villa Auchenibert, près de Killearn, pour F. J. Shand (achevée en 1906).

1905 Salle à manger pour A. S. Ball à Berlin.

1906 Conçoit la nouvelle salle du conseil de la Glasgow School of Art.
Refait les plans de la seconde phase de construction de la Glasgow School of Art (plans achevés en 1907).
Les Mackintosh s'installent au 6 Florentine Terrace.
Dessine la «Dutch Kitchen» (Cuisine hollandaise) pour le Argyle Street Tea Rooms.
Conçoit la villa Mosside (rebaptisée plus tard Cloak), près de Kilmacolm, pour H. B. Collins (modifications apportées en 1912).
Est élu membre du Royal Institute of British Architects.

1907 Dessine la «Oak Room» (Salle en chêne) pour le Ingram Street Tea Rooms.

1909 La seconde phase de construction de la Glasgow School of Art est achevée.
Exposition au Kunstschau de Vienne.

1911 Dessine la «Cloister Room» (Salle du cloître) et le «Chinese Room» (Salon chinois) pour le Ingram Street Tea Rooms.

1913 Mackintosh démissionne de l'agence Honeyman & Keppie.

1914 Les Mackintosh passent une grande partie de l'année à Walberswick dans le Suffolk et réalisent des études de fleurs.

1915 Le couple s'installe à Londres.

1916 Dessine des tissus pour les firmes londoniennes Foxton's et Sefton's.
Reconstruction de la façade et nouvelle décoration intérieure de la villa du 78 Derngate à Northampton pour W. J. Bassett-Lowke (travaux achevés en 1917).

1917 Projet pour la salle dite «The Dug-Out» (L'Abri) pour le Willow Tea Rooms.

1920 Projets de trois ateliers à Chelsea (dont un seul est construit, celui d'Harold Squire).
Projet d'immeuble avec des ateliers pour la Arts League of Service à Chelsea (projet non réalisé).
Projet de théâtre pour Margaret Morris à Chelsea (projet non réalisé).

1923 Les Mackintosh s'installent en France à Port-Vendres.
Mackintosh expose des aquarelles à la Cinquième Exposition Internationale de Chicago et à Londres.

1927 Les Mackintosh retournent à Londres.
L'artiste souffre d'un cancer de la langue.

1928 Mackintosh meurt à Londres le 10 décembre.

1933 Margaret Macdonald meurt à Londres.
Exposition commémorative Mackintosh à Glasgow.

Notes
Anmerkungen

1   Charles Rennie Mackintosh was to change the spelling of his sur-
name several times, from "M'Intosh" to "McIntosh" to "MackIntosh",
eventually settling for the more English version of the name,
Mackintosh, around the time he met the Macdonald sisters.

2   Alistair Moffat (ed.): *Remembering Charles Rennie Mackintosh*, Lanark,
1989, p. 104.

3   Thomas Howarth: *Charles Rennie Mackintosh and the Modern Movement*,
London & New York, 1952, p. 2.

4   Pamela Robertson (ed.): *Charles Rennie Mackintosh: The Architectural
Papers*, Glasgow, 1990, p. 26.

5   Howarth, pp. 9–7.

6   Quote taken from a paper entitled *Architecture* delivered by
Mackintosh in February 1893 to the Glasgow Institute. This part of
the lecture was to some extent plagiarised from J. D. Sedding's essay
"Design"; in: *Arts & Crafts Essays*, London 1893; see: Robertson, p.
207.

7   Anthony Jones: *Charles Rennie Mackintosh*, London, 1990, p. 28.

8   William R. Lethaby: *Architecture, Mysticism and Myth*, published 1891;
David MacGibbon & Thomas Ross: *The Castellated & Domestic Architecture of Scotland*, published 1887–1892.

9   Robertson, p. 52.

10 George Henry and Edward Atkinson Hornel visited Japan together
in 1893/94.

11 Hirokai Kimura & Macmillan, Andrew: "Charles Rennie Mackintosh",
in: *Process Architecture*, No. 50, Tokyo, August 1984, pp. 124–125.

12 Howarth, p. 228.

13 Quote by Osbert Burdett; see: Howarth, p. 227.

14 William Gaunt: *The Pre-Raphaelite Dream*, London, 1943, p. 286.

15 Jones, p. 33.

16 *The Studio*, vol. X, London, 1896, pp. 203–205.

17 For example, the "Gladsmuir" furniture designed c. 1894–1895 which
was shown at the 1896 Arts & Crafts Society Exhibition.

18 Werner J. Schweiger: *Wiener Werkstätte: Design in Vienna 1903–1932*,
London, 1984, p. 17.

19 Contrary to popular belief, not all critics of the exhibition accepted
the Four's work with relish. Ludwig Abels found it "pretty decadent",
while Ludwig Hevesi thought that such interiors were unlivable in
and decried "a simplicity that wallows in its own virtuosity"; see:
Schweiger, p. 18.

20 Hermann Muthesius was sent to Britain in 1896. He and his wife,
Anna, became great friends of the Mackintoshes; indeed, Mackintosh was godfather to their son, Eckart.

21 Hermann Muthesius: *Das Englische Haus*, 2nd ed., Berlin 1909–1911,
vol. I, p. 178.

22 Peter Vergo: "Gustav Klimt's Beethoven Frieze", in: *The Burlington
Magazine*, vol. CXV, London, 1973, pp. 109–113.

23 Howarth, p. 156.

24 Roger Billcliffe: *Charles Rennie Mackintosh: The Complete Furniture,
Furniture Drawings and Interior Designs*, London, 1970, p. 54.

25 Alexander Koch was the publisher of the German art magazine
Deutsche Kunst und Dekoration.

26 Entered under the nom de plume "Der Vogel" (The Bird), the
Mackintoshes' designs for the "Haus eines Kunstfreundes" (House
for an Art Lover) were submitted late and incomplete, and were
thereby formally disqualified from the competition.

27 Jones, p. 61.

28 Howarth, p. 92.

29 Robertson, p. 186.

30 Quote by Walter Blackie; see: *Scottish Art Review*, Special Number,
Glasgow, 1968, p. 7.

31 Moffat, p. 72.

32 Catalogue: *Charles Rennie Mackintosh: Architectural Drawings*,
Hunterian Art Gallery, Glasgow, 1990, p. 26.

33 Moffat, pp. 93–94.

34 Howarth, p. 211.

35 *Our Railways* published in 1922 and *Wireless* published in 1925.

36 Moffat, p. 109.

37 Patrick Nuttgens: *Mackintosh and his Contemporaries in Europe and
America*, London, 1988, p. 23.

38 Howarth, p. 11.

BIBLIOGRAPHY
BIBLIOGRAPHIE

Billcliffe, Roger: *Mackintosh Watercolours*, London, 1979.

Billcliffe, Roger: *Mackintosh Textile Designs*, London, 1982.

Billcliffe, Roger: *Mackintosh Furniture*, Newton Abbot, 1984.

Billcliffe, Roger: *Charles Rennie Mackintosh: The Complete Furniture, Furniture Drawings and Interior Designs*, London, 1986.

Brett, David: *Charles Rennie Mackintosh: The Poetics of Workmanship*, London, 1992.

Buchanan, William (ed.): *Mackintosh's Masterwork, The Glasgow School of Art*, Glasgow, 1989.

Burkhauser, Jude (ed.): *Glasgow Girls, Women in Art and Design 1880–1920*, Edinburgh, 1993.

Cooper, Jackie (ed.): *Mackintosh Architecture*, New York & London, 1984.

Cumming, E.: *Glasgow 1900, Art & Design*, Zwolle, 1993.

Howarth, Thomas: *Charles Rennie Mackintosh and the Modern Movement*, London, 1977.

Jones, Anthony: *Charles Rennie Mackintosh*, New Jersey & London, 1990.

Kimura, Hirokai & Macmillan, Andrew: "Charles Rennie Mackintosh", *Process Architecture*, No. 50, Tokyo, 1984.

Laganá, Guido (ed.): *Charles Rennie Mackintosh (1868–1928)*, Milan, 1988.

Macleod, Robert: *Charles Rennie Mackintosh: Architect and Artist*, London, 1983.

Moffat, Alistair: *Remembering Charles Rennie Mackintosh, An Illustrated Biography*, Lanark, 1989.

Nuttgens, Patrick (ed.): *Mackintosh and His Contemporaries in Europe and America*, London, 1988.

Pevsner, Nikolaus: *Pioneers of Modern Design, From William Morris to Walter Gropius*, London, 1960.

Pevsner, Nikolaus: *Sources of Modern Architecture and Design*, London, 1968.

Robertson, Pamela (ed.): *Charles Rennie Mackintosh: The Architectural Papers*, Oxford, 1990.

CATALOGUES

Mackintosh Flower Drawings, Hunterian Art Gallery, Glasgow, 1988.

Mackintosh and other aspects of the George Smith Collection, Hunterian Art Gallery, Glasgow, 1988.

Charles Rennie Mackintosh at the Hunterian Art Gallery, Hunterian Art Gallery, Glasgow, 1991.

Mackintosh and the Vorticists, The Fine Art Society, London, 1993.

ACKNOWLEDGEMENTS
DANKSAGUNG | REMERCIEMENTS

The publishers would like to express their particular thanks to the following individuals and institutions, all of whom have contributed to the successful realisation of this book:

Der besondere Dank des Verlags geht an die folgenden Personen und Institutionen, die in vielfältiger Weise an der erfolgreichen Realisierung dieses Projekts mitgearbeitet haben:

La maison d'édition tient à remercier les personnes et institutions suivantes qui ont contribué à la réalisation de cet ouvrage:

Douglas M. Annan, T. & R. Annan & Sons Ltd., Glasgow
Roger Billcliffe, Glasgow
Torsten Bröhan, Düsseldorf
Sir Ilay Campbell, Christie's Scotland Ltd., Glasgow
Patricia Douglas, Charles Rennie Mackintosh Society, Glasgow
Anne Ellis, Hill House, Helensburgh
Philippe Garner, Sotheby's, London
Victoria Gibson, Christie's Scotland Ltd., Glasgow
Anne Mulhern, The Willow Tea Rooms, Glasgow
Reverend & Mrs. John Nicol, Bridge of Allan
Josh Parker, Ruchill Street Church Halls, Glasgow
Andrew Patrick, The Fine Art Society, London
Denise Pulford, Hunterian Art Gallery, Glasgow
Peter Reekie, National Trust for Scotland, Edinburgh
Mrs. Riccardo Cornaccio, Killearn
Pamela Robertson, Hunterian Art Gallery, Glasgow
Graham Roxburgh, Craigie Hall, Glasgow
Mrs. Sinclair, Kilmacolm
Dorothy Stewart, Scotland Street School, Glasgow
Edward Synder, Christie's Images, London
Peter Trowles, Glasgow School of Art
Winnie Tyrrell, The Burrell Collection, Glasgow
Jessica White, The British Museum, London
The Royal Highland Fusiliers Museum, Glasgow

CREDITS
BILDNACHWEIS

l. = left | links | à gauche
r. = right | rechts | à droite
t. = top | oben | ci-dessus
c. = centre | Mitte | centre
b. = bottom | unten | ci-dessous
p. = page | Seite | page

p. 2   © Anthony Oliver, London
pp. 6–9   © Photo: T. & R. Annan & Sons, Glasgow
pp. 10–11   Hunterian Art Gallery, University of Glasgow
p. 12   Private Collection
p. 13   Hunterian Art Gallery, University of Glasgow
pp. 14–16   Glasgow Museums: Art Gallery & Museum, Kelvingrove
p. 17   Hunterian Art Gallery, University of Glasgow
p. 18   Glasgow Museums: Art Gallery & Museum, Kelvingrove
p. 19   Hunterian Art Gallery, University of Glasgow
p. 20   Glasgow School of Art, Mackintosh Collection
p. 21   Hunterian Art Gallery, University of Glasgow
p. 22   Deutsche Kunst und Dekoration, 10, 1902, p. 586
p. 23   Österreichisches Museum für angewandte Kunst, Vienna
p. 25 t.   Hunterian Art Gallery, University of Glasgow
p. 25 b.   © Photo: T. & R. Annan & Sons, Glasgow
p. 26   © Photo: T. & R. Annan & Sons, Glasgow
p. 27   © Anthony Oliver, London
p. 28   Hunterian Art Gallery, University of Glasgow
p. 29 t.   © Anthony Oliver, London
p. 29 b.   © Photo: T. & R. Annan & Sons, Glasgow
p. 30   © Anthony Oliver, London
p. 31 t.   © Photo: T. & R. Annan & Sons, Glasgow
p. 31 b.   © Anthony Oliver, London
p. 32   © Anthony Oliver, London
p. 33   Hunterian Art Gallery, University of Glasgow
p. 35   Courtesy Fine Arts Society, London
pp. 36–37   Courtesy Christie's, London
pp. 38–39   Hunterian Art Gallery, University of Glasgow
p. 41   British Museum, London
p. 42   Hunterian Art Gallery, University of Glasgow
p. 43   Glasgow School of Art, Mackintosh Collection
p. 45   © Photo: T. & R. Annan & Sons, Glasgow
p. 46   © Anthony Oliver, London
p. 47   Hunterian Art Gallery, University of Glasgow
p. 48   © Anthony Oliver, London
p. 49 t.   Hunterian Art Gallery, University of Glasgow
p. 49 b.   © Anthony Oliver, London
p. 50   Hunterian Art Gallery, University of Glasgow
p. 51   © Photo: T. & R. Annan & Sons, Glasgow
pp. 52–53   © Anthony Oliver, London
p. 54 t.   © Anthony Oliver, London
p. 54 b.   Glasgow School of Art, Mackintosh Collection
pp. 55–56   © Anthony Oliver, London
pp. 57–58   Glasgow School of Art, Mackintosh Collection
p. 59   © Anthony Oliver, London
p. 60   Glasgow School of Art, Mackintosh Collection
p. 61   © Anthony Oliver, London. Glasgow School of Art, Mackintosh Collection
p. 62 l.   © Anthony Oliver, London. Glasgow School of Art, Mackintosh Collection
p. 62 r.   Hunterian Art Gallery, University of Glasgow
p. 63   © Anthony Oliver, London. Glasgow School of Art, Mackintosh Collection
p. 64   Courtesy Fine Art Society, London
p. 65 t. & c.   The Studio, 39, 1907, p. 34
p. 65 b.   © Photo: T. & R. Annan & Sons, Glasgow
p. 66 t.   Hunterian Art Gallery, University of Glasgow
p. 66 b. l.   Courtesy Christie's, London
p. 66 b. r.   The Studio, 39, 1907, p. 32
p. 67   Courtesy Sotheby's, London
p. 68   © Photo: T. & R. Annan & Sons, Glasgow
p. 69   Hunterian Art Gallery, University of Glasgow
pp. 70–71   © Anthony Oliver, London
pp. 72–73   © Photo: T. & R. Annan & Sons, Glasgow
p. 74   Hunterian Art Gallery, University of Glasgow
p. 75   Hermann Muthesius, Das Englische Haus, 1903, vol. I, p. 186
p. 76   Dekorative Kunst, 4, 1901, p. 175
p. 77   Glasgow School of Art, Mackintosh Collection
p. 78   © Anthony Oliver, London
p. 79 t.   Glasgow School of Art, Mackintosh Collection
p. 79 b.   © Anthony Oliver, London
p. 80 t.   © Photo: T. & R. Annan & Sons, Glasgow

p. 80 b.   Hunterian Art Gallery, University of Glasgow
p. 81   Hunterian Art Gallery, University of Glasgow
p. 82   Courtesy Sotheby's, London
p. 83 t.   Hunterian Art Gallery, University of Glasgow
p. 83 c.   Hunterian Art Gallery, University of Glasgow
p. 83 b.   Courtesy Sotheby's, London
p. 84   Glasgow Museums: Art Gallery & Museum, Kelvingrove
p. 85 t. l.   Courtesy Christie's, London
p. 85 t. r.   Glasgow School of Art, Mackintosh Collection
p. 85 b. l.   Glasgow School of Art, Mackintosh Collection
p. 85 b. r.   Courtesy Torsten Bröhan, Düsseldorf
p. 86   Hunterian Art Gallery, University of Glasgow
p. 87 t.   Hunterian Art Gallery, University of Glasgow
p. 87 b.   © Anthony Oliver, London
pp. 88–91   Hunterian Art Gallery, University of Glasgow
p. 92   Hermann Muthesius, Das Englische Haus, 1903, vol. III, p. 189
p. 93   Courtesy Fine Art Society, London
p. 94   Hunterian Art Gallery, University of Glasgow
p. 95   Deutsche Kunst und Dekoration, 10, 1902, p. 588
p. 96 t.   Courtesy Sotheby's, London
p. 96 b.   Deutsche Kunst und Dekoration, 10, 1902, p. 589
pp. 97–99   Hunterian Art Gallery, University of Glasgow
p. 100   Courtesy Sotheby's, London
p. 101 t.   Courtesy Fine Art Society, London
p. 101 b.   The Studio, 57, 1913, p. 72
pp. 102–106   © Anthony Oliver, London
p. 107   Deutsche Kunst und Dekoration, 15, 1904–05, pp. 337–338
pp. 108–110   © Anthony Oliver, London
p. 111 t.   © Anthony Oliver, London
p. 111 b.   Hunterian Art Gallery, University of Glasgow
p. 112   © Anthony Oliver, London
p. 113   Dekorative Kunst, 12, 1905, p. 258
p. 114 t.   Courtesy Sotheby's, London
p. 114 b.   Glasgow School of Art, Mackintosh Collection
p. 115   Dekorative Kunst, 12, 1905, p. 260
p. 116 t.   Hunterian Art Gallery, University of Glasgow
p. 116 b.   Dekorative Kunst, 12, 1905, p. 261
p. 117   Courtesy Christie's, London
p. 118   Dekorative Kunst, 12, 1905, p. 269
p. 119 t.   © Anthony Oliver, London
p. 119 b.   Hunterian Art Gallery, University of Glasgow
p. 120   Hunterian Art Gallery, University of Glasgow
p. 121   Glasgow School of Art, Mackintosh Collection
p. 122   Deutsche Kunst und Dekoration, 13, 1903–04, p. 246
p. 123 t.   Illustrierte Geschichte des Kunstgewerbes, 1909, vol. II, p. 593
p. 123 b.   Hunterian Art Gallery, University of Glasgow
p. 124   Courtesy Fine Art Society, London
p. 125   © Photo: T. & R. Annan & Sons, Glasgow
p. 126   Hunterian Art Gallery, University of Glasgow
pp. 127–128   Courtesy Fine Art Society, London
p. 129 t.   Studio Year Book of Decorative Arts, 1907, p. 60
p. 129 b.   Hunterian Art Gallery, University of Glasgow
pp. 130–132   © Anthony Oliver, London
p. 133 t.   Hunterian Art Gallery, University of Glasgow
p. 133 b.   © Anthony Oliver, London
p. 134 t.   Hunterian Art Gallery, University of Glasgow
p. 134 b.   © Anthony Oliver, London
pp. 135–136   © Anthony Oliver, London
p. 137 t.   © Anthony Oliver, London
p. 137 b.   Courtesy Christie's, London
pp. 138–141   © Anthony Oliver. Hunterian Art Gallery, University of Glasgow
pp. 142–144   Hunterian Art Gallery, University of Glasgow
p. 145   © Anthony Oliver. Hunterian Art Gallery, University of Glasgow
pp. 146–149   British Museum, London
pp. 150–151   Hunterian Art Gallery, University of Glasgow
p. 152 t.   Courtesy Fine Art Society, London
p. 152 b.   Hunterian Art Gallery, University of Glasgow
pp. 153–157   Hunterian Art Gallery, University of Glasgow
p. 158   Courtesy Christie's, London
p. 161   Courtesy Fine Art Society, London
pp. 162–163   Glasgow School of Art, Mackintosh Collection
p. 164 t. l.   Hunterian Art Gallery, University of Glasgow
p. 164 t. r.   Courtesy Fine Art Society, London
p. 164 b.   Hunterian Art Gallery, University of Glasgow
pp. 165–166   Hunterian Art Gallery, University of Glasgow
p. 167   Glasgow School of Art, Mackintosh Collection